The Proverbs 31 Man and His Woman

Rena Boston

All Scriptures cited are taken from the King James Version of the Bible.

ISBN 978-0-9972297-1-4

For licensing/copyright information, for additional copies, or for use in specialized settings, contact:

Just Writers Publishing Company
Where Fingers Write From The Heart
Round Lake, Illinois 60073
(847) 494-8420 (telephone)
www.justwriters.com
renaboston@comcast.net
justwriters@comcast.net

Table Contents
The Proverbs 31 Man and His Woman

⋘

DEDICATIONS

To God the Father, Jesus Christ His Son,
and the Holy Spirit

To my husband and best friend
James Ranger

To my daughters and confidants
LeTrisha Daniel
Jeanine Joe

To my grandchildren, my heartbeat
Kenneth Daniel Jr.
Kristopher Daniel
Ashley Joe-Fuqua
Kaleb Daniel

I love and appreciate you all!

A Special Dedication

This book is especially dedicated to my friend,

DELOIS S. ROBINSON

for her support and encouragement. Dee is a Proverbs 31 Woman and the wife of Willie Robinson. She consistently extends her heart and hands to help others. Thank you, Dee, for helping me!

Love you girl,
~Rena~

Acknowledgments

In Memory of
Arthur and Virginia Boston

Special Thanks
Bishop Lorenzo L. Kelly
Bishop Carlis L. Moody, Sr.
Mother Mary A. Moody
Dr. Randolph W. Moore
Elder Edward Jackson
Mary Howard
Lisa Laudé-Raymond
Vanessa Johnson-McCoy

To all who encouraged me with your support, I love you very much.

FOREWORD

~≈~

Growing up in Faith Temple Church of God in Christ, you are taught and fed the Word of God. I know that this was my experience in that church. It is where I encountered the Lord like never before. He showed me things that blew my mind through His Word. He opened my spiritual eyes to see His Word and meaning more clearly.

It has been almost forty years since I left Faith Temple to start a church in another state, and I am happy to see that the great legacy of the church is still going forth through this young lady.

She has taken this very familiar scripture and has expounded on it like Ive never heard before. We see Proverbs 31 in one way, and she totally puts another aspect on it and you can see it so clearly.

I encourage you to open your spiritual eyes to see this meaning of Proverbs 31. The way she explains it has opened me up to another dimension of this scripture. I thank God that I read this book and have put it on my list as a Bible study class.

Bishop Lorenzo L. Kelly
Prelate South Dakota Jurisdiction, Church of God in Christ
Pastor & Founder, Faith Temple Church of God in Christ, Rapid City, South Dakota

INTRODUCTION

⁊

All of the teachings I have ever heard on Proverbs 31 have applied to the woman. It was usually neatly wrapped in The Proverbs 31 Woman, until one day God challenged me, and oh, what a challenge. It was the birth of this book, *The Proverbs 31 Man and His Woman*.

It was early morning, and the sun was already shinning brightly through the patio glass doors. I sat at the kitchen table having my morning devotion and sipping my oversized cup of coffee. I sat comfortably reading my Bible.

While reading a chapter in the Book of Proverbs, it happened. The Lord spoke to my heart. He asked me an extremely pointed question. Rena, what kind of man would it take to live happily with a Proverbs 31 Woman? I did not respond as quickly as I would have, if one of my friends had asked me that question. I knew I had to respond to God with an *insightful* answer. Right or wrong, I had to give Him my best answer.

I turned the pages of my Bible to Chapter 31 of Proverbs and scanned the beginning of the chapter. Knowing I had the answer, I smiled and responded, A King or a Prince is the kind of man who will make a Proverbs 31 Woman happy. God so sweetly responded to my proud *intellectual* answer. He said, Yes, thats part of the answer. My eyebrows raised and my mind retorted, Only part?

When I snapped out of my thoughts, I realized that there was an overwhelming silence. It was as if He was waiting for the rest of my answer. I returned to the beginning of Chapter 31, and continued reading. Being a woman, wife, mother, and grandmother, I knew I was on point this time. Surely, this will complete the answer. I said to the Lord, The man whose mother has taught him about women.I was instantly deflated. I wasnt as smart as Id thought. The Lord wanted to teach me a lesson. Again, He so sweetly responded to my answer. He said, Its that also, but it is so much more. Go to Chapter One. I turned the pages to Chapter 1 and He continued, Rena, the man who **_listens_**, **_learns_**, and **_lives_** by the principles contained in the Book of Proverbs, from Chapter 1 through Chapter 31, will be a suitable match for a Proverbs 31 Woman. He must pass the tests of life contained in the Book of Proverbs, to be equipped for the Proverbs 31 Woman. He doesnt need a perfect score, but he must go through the process successfully. I charge you, to pass it on. Wow! I sat numb; not knowing how or what to do. It was exasperating. The conversation had already taken all I had to offer out of me. There was a question in my head, but I was not going to ask it. How do I, a woman, deliver this message successfully to men?

After months of communing with the Lord about my assigned task, I became absolutely convinced that Proverbs 31 was *not* as much about the Woman, as it was about the Man. The Author is a King. His name means Devoted to God He is rehearsing in writing, a prophecy that his mother taught him. Prophecies foretell the future. She was preparing him for life. She addresses the standard of living appropriate for kings and princes. She made her illustration practical. He was a king, so he could easily relate to her examples. She reminds him of the characteristics and strengths of kings and princes. Then she appeals to his heart, and his love for people. Lastly, she provides specific and detailed descriptions of the Woman, who would make a good wife. She starts with a thought-provoking rhetorical question; then she proceeds to answer the question, describing the Woman. This is the Woman, to whom this Man must prepare himself to marry.

TODAYS TRAINING

WILL PRODUCE

TOMORROWS RESULTS!

PROVERBS
The Purpose and Process

⁓

The Book of Proverbs, the 20th Book of the Bible, is not just a book of wise sayings. It is a book filled with principles for living a victorious life. Many of the Proverbs were written by Solomon, the third King of Israel and the wisest man ever lived. God gave him divine wisdom and great understanding. His writings are reflective of Gods divine wisdom, and the wisdom taught to him by his dad, King David.

The King James Version of the Bible is used throughout this book.

One of the greatest lessons King Solomons life teaches us is, Wisdom is not beneficial unless it is applied.

Most of my life, fear and low self-esteem held me captive in school, church, or just at a gathering. When a question was asked, I would know with a certainty that I knew the answer, but I would not open my mouth. And when the answer given was also my answer, I plunged deeper into the claws of fear and low self-esteem. The knowledge did not benefit me, because I did not open my mouth. Likewise, wisdom is only beneficial when it is applied.

If we follow the principles contained in the Book of Proverbs, we can live victoriously. The Book of Proverbs is a Training Manual. It contains instructions for handling every type of situation in life. Here we are, thousands of years after it was written, and we can still live our lives by the instructions contained in it.

Solomon begins his training by stating the objectives of the training. The training is designed to impact the body, soul, and spirit of man. He desires to accomplish four major goals:

PROVERBS 1:2-4	
! To **know** wisdom and understanding	~get it in your head *(Body)*
! To **perceive** the words of understanding	~get it in your mind *(Soul)*
! To **receive** the instruction of wisdom, justice, judgment, and equity	~get it in your heart *(Spirit)*
! To **give** subtlety to the simple, to the young man knowledge and discretion	~after you have learned, teach others *(Outreach)*

To some, these may seem like easily obtainable objectives, but dont be fooled. This is a life long training session. Certain areas of training are so critical that they are repeated throughout the manual. The manual also includes different levels of wisdom and instructions for all the issues of life.

The introduction opens with a discussion regarding the foundation of life, which starts with God. All aspects of a successful life are built on God, the foundation. The manual states, *The fear of the Lord is the beginning of knowledge: but fools despise wisdom and instruction (Proverbs 1:7).*

The word fear can be interchanged with reverence. The person who reverences God has obtained the highest level of knowledge. This reverence is the pathway and the very essence of learning wisdom, understanding, and knowledge. It starts at the top with God and trickles down. The reverence of God brings wisdom; thus, wisdom comes from God. We, who are wise, are responsible for allowing wisdom to overflow to others, by reaching and teaching.

Faith in God guides us through the paths of this life, and His Word helps us see more clearly, the condition of our hearts and the world. His Word illuminates and equips us to distinguish between right and wrong.

Although God was explicit with me regarding the contents of the Book of Proverbs, I didnt know where to begin. I only knew that the title of the book was, The Proverbs 31 Man and His Woman.

I did the only thing I could do. I looked to God through His Word for guidance. I read Chapter 31 repeatedly and meditated on it. Then the words My Son illuminated. I saw it clearly. When his mother was giving him instructions, she first addressed him as My Son. I began to peruse the pages of the Book of Proverbs. I wanted to see how many times the phrase My Son was used at the beginning of a sentence with instructions following it. I discovered 17 times. This salutation opened the door to the topics for the training sessions. Even though the phrase My Son was literal, it also applies to men in general.

The Proverbs 31 Man and His Woman summarizes the 17 lessons. And it provides every man with a handy manual to build his legacy of instructions. In certain situations I have inserted the actual scripture, rather than a summary, because an interpretation would dilute the direct and impactful message.

I then decided to research the biblical meaning of the number 17. It was a joyous surprise to learn that 17 represented,

Complete and Total Victory and Perfection of Spiritual Order. I was intrigued. I realized that a great work was before me.

Chapters Eight through Twenty-two did not contain the phrase My Son at the beginning of a sentence with instructions following it, so I sought to further understand. There were 15 chapters from eight to twenty-two. I looked up the biblical meaning of the number 15. The number 15 means, New Direction in Life and Symbolizes Rest, which come After Deliverance.

Wow! Reading the meaning of number 15 gave me great anticipation. I could barely wait to read the contents of those chapters. The developing of this book was becoming more and more interesting. I thought, In school, subjects are classified as major and minor. I asked myself, Is it possible that when the major lessons of life are learned, the minor lessons will instinctively become the new way of life? I should not have been surprised to learn that those chapters repeated a lot of the lessons previously taught. Nevertheless, these lessons were needful because they reinforced the instructions, regarding the critical issues of life and their pitfalls.

I viewed these chapters like the **branches** of life. After learning and applying the major lessons, these lessons create an easier transition into the new path of life. Thus, these chapters are Independent Studies. The Independent Studies help every man identify the type of man he is. They also provide the fundamental information needed to develop into the man he desires to become.

We can conclude that every son who successfully _listens_, _learns_, and _lives_ by these 17 lessons, will be completely equipped to live in total victory with a wife as described in Proverbs 31. No intimidation or threat, just joy!

OVERVIEW

⁓

Each chapter contained in this book coincides with a specific Proverbs Chapter presented in a sequential chapter order. You may choose to read the Proverbs chapter, which coincides with each chapter contained in this training manual. However, since some of the Proverbs contain more than one set of instructions, each one is presented in a separate chapter within the book.

At the beginning of Chapters 1 through 12, 14 through 17, and 19, the main Scripture is presented and the summary of the chapter follows it.

Chapters 13, 18, and 20 cover Proverbs Chapters 8 through 22, 25 through 26, and 28 through 30 and are designed as Independent Studies. However, the core and critical elements of these chapters have been highlighted.

Chapter 21 covers Proverbs 31 in its entirety. Each verse of Proverbs 31 is used to describe and discuss both the Proverbs 31 Man and His Woman. This is done separately; therefore, each verse is cited twice.

Dare to revolutionize your perspective!

LISTEN

LEARN

LIVE

CHAPTER 1

THE FOUNDATION
LESSON: INSTRUCTION AND LAW

My son, hear the instruction of thy father, and forsake not the law of thy mother: For they shall be an ornament of grace unto thy head, and chains about thy neck.
Proverbs 1:8-9

Out of the seventeen lessons, this is the only one where the complete instructions are contained within the scripture. No examples were given, just a simple command to hear dads instruction and hold onto moms law.

Instruction means to teach, train, guide, and point to show the direction to take. The Hebrew meaning of *instruction* is more than just *law*. It means to shoot out the hand as pointing, to show, indicate, teach, to lay foundations, to sprinkle, to water, and to shoot as an arrow. These instructions pertain to moral, social and spiritual behaviors.

A wise dad grooms a wise son. A wise dad will lead and provide for his family. He will love his wife and instruct his children. He will direct the paths of his family in the right way. He will guide them in truth. Throughout Solomons instructions, he illustrates life issues, applies wise solutions, and presents the pros and cons of unwise decisions. He provides a practical walk-through of each situation and its end results.

The *law* is simply, a wise mom carrying out or enforcing the instructions dad has given. She is the epitome of the *Law of Love* and the *Fountain of Life.* When Dad says, Do. Dont do, Mom says, Let me show you how. The Law is used to implement, monitor, and disciple with hands-on application, the instructions that have been given.

Mom takes the instructions and nourishes her son with them. Her goal is to establish in her son, the spiritual and natural aspects of the instructions. The *law* is Training-In-Action.Mom is the channel that produces practical application. Dad gives his son instructions, and his son learns the practical meaning of Dads instructions while sitting on Moms knees, or following her around throughout the day.

The foundation of all good instructions and laws is **wisdom.**

CHAPTER 2

THE INVITATION
LESSON: GANGS, ROBBERY, AND MURDER

My son, if sinners entice thee, consent thou not.
Proverbs 1:10

After the foundation has been established, the first practical lesson the son is taught pertains to his friends and associates. He is **cautioned** not to accept, or be enticed by invitations from those whose standard *for* living conflicts with his.

One of the most liberating revelations Ive heard about *sinners,* came from my pastor, Bishop Carlis L. Moody, Sr., many years ago. He said, Why are you so surprised at whats happening in the world? Sinners do, what sinners do, they sin. It was simple, yet so profound. Sinners operate according to their nature and character.

Solomon could not have said it any clearer. Son, dont join your hand or your heart with sinners. Beware of all their invitations! If they say,

1.   Come with us, let us ambush and kill someone,
2.   Let us rape the innocent,
3.   Let us rob the houses of the wealthy,
4.   Give us your money, so we can put it in our purse
     Son, dont do it! Dont consent to any of it!

Their appetite is different from yours. You desire to do what is right, which is to live peaceably and operate in truth. If you partake of the sinners menu, it will stimulate an appetite that is contrary to yours.

My eldest grandson was not given sweets from infancy until age four or five. The first time he tasted a sweet treat, he spat it out. It was distasteful. The next time, he disliked only a portion of it. However, by the third or fourth time, he was consuming whatever sweets were given to him. Today, it is still an enemy that he is fighting.

There are so many degrees of *loss of control* that it is frightening. Thats why it is so important for us to *keep our appetites keen to the fruit of truth and right living.*

I do not deny, that sin is enjoyable for a while. Many victims have said, Ill try it once (whatever it is). Then oops! Its too late. They liked it. The more they did it, the more they were controlled by it. Their appetite changed. At first sin looks good. Its package is enticing. It appears to bring good results. It gives its victims boldness. Before you realize what has happened, you have lost yourself. Someone once said, Sin will take you further than you want to go, and keep you longer than you want to stay. You are hooked, but not on drugs, gangs, or the like; you are hooked on sin. And sinners do, what sinners do, drugs, gangs, and the like.

There is nothing new under the sun. Every temptation that exists in the world is common to everyone. However, it alters its face based on the weakness of each individual. Temptation customizes itself for its victim. Regardless of the form temptation comes in, God has made provision for each of us to overcome it. God is always present to help us when we face temptation and He promises to help us, if we ask Him.

The temporary pleasure that sin offers is not worth your life. It is deceptive. Do not yield to the temptation. It is the yielding that brings sin, and sin brings death. RSVP your invitation with, Will Not Attend!

CHAPTER 3

SINKING GROUND
――――――――――∘∘∘⟶∘∘∘――――――――――
LESSON: WATCH YOUR WALK

My son, walk not thou in the way with them; refrain thy foot from their path: For their feet run to evil, and make haste to shed blood. **Proverbs 1:15-16**

This segment of your training is an expansion and reinforcement of your previous lesson. You were previously told not to accept their invitations. At this level, your two-fold instructions are more intense, ***Dont walk with them and Refrain thy foot from their path.***

This lesson is intense because when you separate yourself, you will be judged and may even be attacked. I understand that you want people to like you. I understand that you want to be accepted. But I must remind you that you are the one, who knows your true value. Dont settle for less. You may be isolated and mocked, but it does not change who you are.

When you dont comply with their request to walk with them, they may accuse you of thinking that you are better than they. Dont respond, but know that you are better. Dont allow others to validate you. Validate yourself. Tell others about the champion within you.

Whether subliminal, oral, or written, you will receive an invitation from them. They want as many as possible to join them. There will be collateral damage and it just might be YOU.

Dont think it ends with you saying, No once or even twice. They have already sent you four invitations. They have invited you to join their gang, participate in a robbery, engage in a rape, and commit murder. They will keep trying until they find the temptation you wont resist. Their identity is in the things they do. It is their character. They will do whatever it takes to promote their agenda. *Their hunger for power is satisfied at the demise of another.*

In the previous lesson, you were **cautioned** not to accept the invitation. Now you are being **warned** not to even associate casually with them. Do not walk with them. It has been said, Association brings about assimilation! Most people will look at the group you associate with and surmise what type and caliber of person you are.

My son, dont let your name be associated with those who run to evil. They dont think twice about shedding blood, even their own. They are people who choose to be ignorant, disrespectful, and foolish, separate from them. When it is all said and done, when they are alone, fear will grip them and their destruction will come as a whirlwind. They will not know what hit them. The lack of wisdom will destroy them.

You are able to refrain from yielding to the temptation, although you may be struggling with it. Like every person alive, you want to be accepted. You want to be a part. You ask yourself, Should I or Shouldnt I? Know for certain, if you walk with them, you are walking away, from the blessings of your life. There are two paths to walk, the path of life, and the path of death, you must choose!

CHAPTER 4

LISTEN WITH YOUR HEART

LESSON: SEEK AND SEARCH

*My son, if thou wilt receive my words, and hide my
commandments with thee; So that thou incline thine ear
unto wisdom, and apply thine heart to understanding; Yea,
if thou criest after knowledge, and liftest up thy voice for
understanding; If thou seekest her as silver, and searchest for
her as for hid treasures; Then shalt thou understand the fear of
the Lord, and find the knowledge of God.*
Proverbs 2:1-5

Out of the seventeen training sessions, this one contains the
most verses and the longest salutation introducing the training
topic. It reiterates the four main goals, which were introduced at
the beginning of the training:

! To **know** wisdom and understanding	~get it in your head *(Body)*
! To **perceive** the words of understanding	~get it in your mind *(Soul)*
! To **receive** the instruction of wisdom, justice, judgment, and equity	~get it in your heart *(Spirit)*
! To **give** subtlety to the simple, to the young man knowledge and discretion	~after you have learned, teach others *(Outreach)*

Once you accomplish these goals, you will understand the importance of reverencing God. You wouldve obtained the knowledge of God, which is the foundation of wisdom.

My son, listen and learn! You dont know everything. The application of this lesson requires two members of your body, your ears and your heart. Your ears and your heart are essential to successfully complete the Proverbs 31 Mans Training.

You must listen with your heart as you move forward in your treasure hut. Wisdom is a treasure that you must seek and search out. Wisdom doesnt just appear on the scene. You must seek it as you would a hidden treasure. Once you get it you must use it, otherwise, it is the same as not having it at all. God gives wisdom. It is essential that you discern the depths of your life situations, because they can be deceptive.

All of my life, I believed that we obtain knowledge first, then understanding, and finally the wisdom to apply the former two. Some of you were probably taught the same thing. However, King Solomon, the wisest man who ever lived, presents the sequence of character development as, wisdom, understanding, and then knowledge. Indulge me! I was facing another challenge and I needed help. After meditating and seeking God for an understanding, my spirit finally relaxed. You may not agree and I respect your position. However, this is how my spirit dissected the challenge.

First, I accepted the order presented by the wisest man ever lived, over the way I was taught. Secondly, there is both worldly wisdom and godly wisdom. Divine wisdom starts with God and goes from the top to the bottom. Worldly wisdom is inverted and goes from the bottom to the top. We deceive ourselves if we think we have arrived because we possess the wisdom of this world.

This is a segment of the same lifelong fight between the flesh and the spirit.

Wisdom is the principal thing. With wisdom comes right judgments, equity, discretion and protection. It enables you to choose right from wrong. As taught in Lesson Two, if you are enticed, wisdom strengthens you to say, No Understanding and knowledge follow wisdom. *You dont have to be book-smart to be wise.*

Wisdom protects you from the negative influence of those who are evil. Wisdom protects you from the enticements of the immoral woman, who flatters with her words. The Proverbs 31 Man will recognize that the woman described in this chapter is not the woman for him. She has turned her back on God, and no longer entertains the instruction of her father, or the law of her mother. She is using her body in ways she was warned against. Wisdom not only enables you to make the right choices in life, but it affects all aspects of life; what you say, do and believe.

Wisdom is not a once-and-for-all achievement. It is a life-long process. We can see it in the Proverbs. At each level of a life situation, a new level of wisdom is presented. Wisdom grows in our hearts at the levels of understanding and knowledge we have attained.

Wisdom will help you:

■ Detect Evil Motives
■ Evaluate Actions
■ Identify Consequences

CHAPTER 5

INSTANT RECALL

LESSON: MERCY, TRUTH, and TRUST

My son, forget not my law; but let thine heart keep my commandments: For length of days, and long life, and peace, shall they add to thee.
Proverbs 3:1-2

If you are going to forget anything, dont let it be wisdom. All aspects of wisdom are valuable. Wisdom keeps you, it preserves you, and it protects you. You cant afford to forget or forsake her.

If you live and operate in wisdom, your days will be lengthened, giving you long life and peace. Purpose not to become a mean, old, judgmental human being. Long life loses its value if you cant enjoy it in peace!

There are characteristics of life that you must retain regardless to your path in life. These characteristics are: mercy, truth and trust. Mercy and truth give you favor and good understanding with God and man. However, your trust for your path in life should whole-heartedly be in God. You should not trust yourself or others to lead you to the place where you were destined to go. You should be open to wise counsel, but ultimately, you must totally trust God to lead you. Dont be a know-it-all and get hung by your foolish ideas. Wisdom will open doors for you that you cannot open for yourself.

Your decision to walk through an open door is yours alone. However, you must make a decision to honor God. Since He supplies all of your needs, it is reasonable to honor Him in all that you do. You cant pay God for His goodness to you, but you can honor Him with the first fruit of all your increase. Make God the priority in your life. Give Him the first of your life and all your increase.

Even during times when training is not being given, you must continue practicing that which you were previously taught.

CHAPTER 6

OUCH

LESSON: CHASTISEMENT AND CORRECTION

My son, despise not the chastening of the Lord; neither be weary of his correction: For whom the Lord loveth he correcteth; even as a father the son in whom he delighteth.
Proverbs 3:11-12

Chastisement and correction are other methods of teaching and training. These words are also used in reference to discipline. Back in-the-day, it was simply called a Beat Down. You were beaten. I dare use that term today, because it would be considered abuse. Since spanking is an acceptable term, I will use spanking.

My son, Im giving you everything that is within me. Im giving you the things my father taught me, and the things I learned the hard way. Do yourself a favor. Maintain a teachable spirit. Dont think you wont make mistakes, or purposefully make wrong choices, because you will. Yet, you can rise above them. One thing is sure my son, there are consequences to all of your actions, good, bad, and indifferent.

When we were young, we made fun of our parents and the things they said while beating us. They would say, This hurts me more than it hurts you. My son, after years of living, I can now make sense of that statement. As a child, feeling the pain of the spanking made the statement sound ludicrous. However, the years have brought an understanding. Like God, it hurt them more because their hearts were conditioned to only do good for us. Yet, because we strayed, they had to implement the correction needed to get us back on track. Therefore, it hurt them more, but not the physical pain; it was the pain in their heart.

God does not desire to inflict pain upon us. However, when we stray, he loves us enough to chastise and correct us, and I believe it hurts His heart. Nevertheless, the goal is to develop the character needed to have a successful life.

In this lesson, a segment of Lesson 5 is being repeated, Length of days is in the right hand of wisdom and riches and honor are in the left hand of wisdom. The ways of wisdom are pleasant, and the paths of wisdom are filled with peace. Wisdom is a tree of life, and everyone that has wisdom is happy. Listen! There is no get-rich-quick scheme that offers what wisdom offers.

When the times of your chastisement and correction come, receive it gracefully. Know that it is for your good, and it hurts God more than it hurts you.

CHAPTER 7

THE ADDITIVE

LESSON: DISCRETION

My son, let not them depart from thine eyes: keep sound wisdom and discretion: So shall they be life unto thy soul, and grace to thy neck. Proverbs 3:21-22

Like the blood relationship between siblings, there is a direct correlation between discretion and wisdom. Discretion would be referred to as the first cousin of wisdom. They go hand in hand. Discretion is the ability to make choices and decisions. And wisdom is the ability to make sure they are the right choices and decisions. Dont be caught without discretion and wisdom. To pass the Proverbs test, you need both of them.

Dont think just because you did something in secret, it is not seen. Havent you heard, Whats done in the dark will come to the light! It is always seen. God sees, but even that is not the critical part. It is critical that *discretion* becomes as much a part of your character as wisdom.

Discretion and wisdom will keep the noose off of your neck. They enable you to walk and not stumble. They free you from having to constantly look over your shoulder. Even though discretion and wisdom work well together, you can apply discretion to a situation without using wisdom. An example of discretion and wisdom working together: Discretion ensures that you get your proper amount of sleep by making the decision to go to bed at a reasonable hour. Wisdom ensures that your sleep is peaceful because all your decisions of the day have been right ones.

Discretion and wisdom will help you treat people right. You wont misuse your power or authority. You will avoid the ways of an oppressor. You will fight if necessary, but you will not fight when there is no valid cause. They help you to be a good neighbor. You dont lurk in the dark, waiting to do others wrong.

Even without natural strength, you are a powerful man when you are guided by wisdom and discretion. You will walk and not stumble. When negative things start to happen, and everyone around you becomes fearful, you will laugh in the face of fear, because you have been fortified with that which is good and right. Keep your attention on God and hold fast to the confidence that you have in Him. You will be able to sleep, while others are pacing the floor. God promised to bless your house, so choose to do good all the days of your life.

If you retain wisdom and discretion in your heart, you will inherit glory.

CHAPTER 8

THE LEGACY

LESSON: DEDICATE YOURSELF COMPLETELY

My son, attend to my words; incline thine ear unto my sayings.
Proverbs 4:20

In this session, the scholar speaks to any child who is willing to hear what he has to say. He temporarily deviates from his regular training session to have a rap session with the children. He returns his attention to his son in verse twenty, where he simply says, Listen and Learn!

As he sits and talks with the children, he begins by telling them about his upbringing. He talks of his fathers teachings. He rehearses in their ears, the things his father told him. However, the first thing he requested from the children was that they listen to the instructions and pay close attention. He wanted their undivided attention so they could get an understanding, and never turn their backs on their teachings.

In the midst of his training, the scholar, Solomon, takes a moment to reminisce on what his dad had taught him. He recalls his dads teachings, because this character development training didnt start with him. It was what he was taught. This was his legacy. His father taught him, and the father before him, from generation-to-generation. The teachings he received had such an impact on his life that when God asked what he wanted, he asked for wisdom.

He begins his testimony:

For I was my fathers son, tender and only beloved in the sight of my mother. He taught me also, and said unto me, Let thine heart retain my words: keep my commandments, and live. Get wisdom, get understanding: forget it not; neither decline from the words of my mouth. Forsake her not, and she shall preserve thee: love her, and she shall keep thee. Wisdom is the principal thing; therefore get wisdom: and with all thy getting get understanding. Exalt her, and she shall promote thee: she shall bring thee to honour, when thou dost embrace her. She shall give to thine head an ornament of grace: a crown of glory shall she deliver to thee.

Hear, O my son, and receive my sayings; and the years of thy life shall be many. I have taught thee in the way of wisdom; I have led thee in right paths. When thou goest, thy steps shall not be straitened; and when thou runnest, thou shalt not stumble. Take fast hold of instruction; let her not go: keep her; for she is thy life. Enter not into the path of the wicked, and go not in the way of evil men. Avoid it, pass not by it, turn from it, and pass away. For they sleep not, except they have done mischief; and their sleep is taken away, unless they cause some to fall. For they eat the bread of wickedness, and drink the wine of violence. But the path of the just is as the shining light, that shineth more and more unto the perfect day. The way of the wicked is as darkness: they know not at what they stumble. (Proverbs 4:3-19)

I reiterate, Solomon received divine wisdom from God, but his father, King David, taught him wisdom as a child. He grew up knowing what wisdom looked like. I believe his upbringing made his heart tender towards God. I also believe it was his upbringing that caused him to ask God for wisdom, when he was given carte blanche. In his testimony above, he said his father not only taught him, but he led him also. This is so critical. Today, many sons are chatting the old saying, *What you are doing speaks so loudly, I cant hear what you are saying!* Fathers must practice what they preach. They must be the living example of their words!

His attention returns to his son and the training session begins (Proverbs 4:20). First, he captured his ears; then in the next six verses he encourages his son to preserve every major part of the body. He addresses each of them separately; the eyes, heart, mouth, lips, eyelids, and feet. It is apparent that the issues of life can derive from any member of our body. Offenses can result from what you heard, saw, said, visited, and even contemplated.

The heart is the most critical member. It is the nucleus of your affections. You must make sure you love what is right. The impact of the issues in life rests with the heart. Guard your heart against evil. Seek to know what is in your heart. Look at the things you cultivate, carry around, and even nurse in your heart. Can they cause you heart problems? You must examine your heart daily. You are to protect your heart at all cost. Your heart determines the course of your life. It also determines the boundaries of your life; where you will go and how far. You can accomplish much and achieve many things, but if it is outside of the Purpose for which you were designed, you have missed the mark. Go back and re-examine your heart.

Protecting your heart, protects your actions, and ensures that you make the right choices.

CHAPTER 9

GREENER PASTURE

LESSON: SEXUAL SINS

My son, attend unto my wisdom, and bow thine ear to my understanding: That thou mayest regard discretion, and that thy lips may keep knowledge.
Proverbs 5:1-2

A strong foundation of instructions has been laid. He now introduces the weightier matters, a woman who is prostituting herself. The question is, Can you pass the test? The woman is promiscuous and lewd. Potentially, she is enemy number one to the male species. Up to this point, we have dealt with your inner self, friends, associates, habits, wrongdoings, and so much more. All of those areas need to be settled in order to move on, and remain victorious.

Oh, the woman, that beautiful and lustrous creature. She eats, wipes her mouth, and asks for more. Dont let her eat you alive. She will eat you for breakfast, regurgitate and swallow you for lunch, and throw you in the trash at dinner. She will use all you have to offer, and leave you limp and lifeless. Yet, her lips are as sweet as a honeycomb, and the words of her mouth are smoother than oil.

Her ways are moveable and you cannot know them. She will reveal the persona you want to see, but its not who she is. She changes for convenience. You will meet her sooner or later, but dont go near her. Beware! Be Cautious! Be Alert! When you are introduced to her, let discretion preserve you. Dont be smitten. Dont yield to her outward beauty.

Dont go near the doors to her house. Her name is over the door, but if you look closer youll see that it is not her name at all. The words read, Danger! Danger! She is deadly, and if you regard not discretion you will die a horrible death. The things you were taught will die, along with the blessings and honor you have known. If you allow yourself to be consumed by her, you will join the others who said, *How have I hated instruction, and my heart despised reproof; And have not obeyed the voice of my teachers, nor inclined mine ear to them that instructed me! (Proverbs 5:12-13).*

You must answer your own question, and still resolve to help others. You hope others will learn from you, the things you learned the hard way. You tell the married man, Drink waters out of your own cistern which is to say, Stay faithful to your wife. Dont destroy your family. Enjoy her without guilt, and rejoice with her. Have fun with her. It could not be said any better than stated, *Let her be as the loving hind and pleasant roe; let her breasts satisfy thee at all times; and be thou ravished always with her love (Proverbs 5:19).*

Dont destroy your life with a prostitute. Your wife has what you need. Your fulfillment and satisfaction are within your marriage. Dont live or die like a man who did not receive the legacy of instructions. ***The price of a prostitute is not monetary; it is a destroyed life!***

CHAPTER 10

THE REVERSAL
——————◦◦◦◦◦——————

LESSON: WARNINGS AGAINST FOOLISHNESS

My son, if thou be surety for thy friend, if thou hast stricken
thy hand with a stranger, Thou art snared with the words of
thy mouth, thou art taken with the words of thy mouth.
Proverbs 6:1-2

Warnings are good and most helpful when you get them in advance of your actions. Theres hope that you will take heed. Still some warnings given after you have done the deed can enable you to reverse your action, and even separate yourself from it.

In this session, you will learn about co-signing, laziness, and the things God hates. However, before he introduces those areas, he presents one of the most important lessons of life. The scholar said, You must guard your mouth and watch the words that flow from your lips. What you say can liberate or imprison you.

The lesson continues. Co-signing for another persons debt is not wise. You are not using the wisdom, which was imparted to you. You thought youd received and embraced wisdom. You were certain that you would not participate in foolish and empty things. Nevertheless, you find yourself in a place where you never thought you would be. You not only co-signed a debt for someone you believed was your friend, but you also made a pledge with a stranger. You didnt even know the character of this stranger; yet, your name and reputation are on the line, because you vouched for them. You may have confused kindness and generosity with irresponsibility.

Dont allow others to make you feel guilty about your success. Guilt will make you do foolish things just to prove them wrong. You will find yourself in financial bondage. You will be *locked down* and *locked out,* because co-signing and pledging can do that to you.

The scholar encourages you to reverse the situation. This is what you must do. You cannot delay. You must do it now. Dont take a nap. Dont go to bed. Dont even close your eyes. Go find yourself, remove the noose from off your neck and the band off of your shoulder. Ask your friend to pay the debt, so you can be released. Set yourself free. You called him friend. You must make sure he is a friend. Your friendship must be a 2-way street. You know your motives and why you called him friend, now go and make sure he is your friend. There are signs. There are things friends will do and will not do for the sake of the friendship. As you examine your relationship with your friend, examine yourself.

You must stand and be a man. You cannot be lazy. You must have insight and foresight. Your actions must exceed the actions of the ant. Look at yourself through the eyes of the ant. They have no teacher; yet, their work ethics, diligence, and stewardship far exceed yours.

You have a teacher. You have a trainer. You have a leader and written resources; yet, your actions are questionable. The scholar said, Listen, you cannot sleep all day; buy everything you want; be naughty; do wicked things; talk with your eyes, feet, and fingers; and not end up broken spiritually and naturally.

Since the basic principles of wisdom did not sustain you, I must now teach you on a specific level and at a slower pace. Lets start with the things God hates. When our *Legacy of Instructions* started, you were told God was the foundation of this Legacy. He reigns and sets the standards that you live by. Some specific things God hates are: a proud look, a lying tongue, hands that shed innocent blood, a heart that devise wicked imaginations, feet that are swift in running to mischief, and a false witness that speaks lies (Proverbs 6:17-19a).

All of these areas were covered in earlier sessions; yet, it is critical that they be repeated. Also, we cant forget the thing, which is an abomination to God; and that is, The person who sows discord among brethren (Proverbs 6:19b). Dont forget, even your prayers can be hindered or ineffective when there is not a life of grace between you and your wife (1 Peter 3:7).

A troublemaker who causes disagreements between people is not the person you want to be. Though unwise, your co-signing and pledging were almost understandable. Because they were probably done with the best intentions, but discord causes heart disease. However, co-signing and pledging, along with a whisperer, have proven to be great separators of friends and family.

Then there is the laziness. Any lazy and careless living must be reversed to reflect the wisdom you have been taught. *When wisdom prevails all of the things God hates, diminishes.*

We must be wise. Wisdom is the vehicle, which takes us to our destiny!

CHAPTER 11

SNEAKING AND PEEKING

LESSON: ADULTERY

My son, keep thy fathers commandment, and forsake not the law of thy mother: Bind them continually upon thine heart, and tie them about thy neck.
Proverbs 6:20-21

When these lessons are really learned and settled in your heart, wisdom works continuously. It will lead you when you walk. It will keep you when you sleep. And it will talk to you when you are awake.

In this lesson, you are reminded that your fathers commandment is a lamp unto your feet and your mothers law is the light unto your path. Nevertheless, a reprimand, a rebuke, or a reminder of the instructions given to you, is a way of life. Repetition! Repetition! Repetition! Get use to it! The same instructions will be given to you repeatedly, each time with a new twist.

The prostitute and lewd women were previously discussed. Yet, the subject comes up again, but this time in reference to the adulterous woman. You have been warned about the flattery of the tongue. You have been cautioned not to lust after her beauty. You were told about the batting of her eyelids. Listen closely, this is the result of yielding to these temptations: For by means of a whorish woman, a man is brought to a piece of bread (Proverbs

6:26a). This should scare you, but if you think thats bad, look at the adulteress.

The adulteress will **hunt** for the precious life. (Proverbs 6:26b) She is on the prowl. The question is: Will you be caught? If you are living a clean and precious life, you are her number one candidate. You dont even have to submit a resumé. She will hunt until she finds you. It wont be hard for her to find you. There is a clean scent and an aura that you maintain, which reveal that you are a precious life. She is seeking you, the cream of the crop!

The main objective of this lesson is for you to realize, and know with certainty, that your life is precious. Once you know how valuable you are, chances are slim that you will be caught in her snares. She is shrewd. Things will begin innocently. Her pretense of innocence will appear as clean as the precious life you are living. The lightheartedness of your interactions will keep you smiling. The reasonableness of having a platonic friend goes unnoticed. Nevertheless, you were taught that dealing with these types of women was like placing fire in your bosom, and walking on hot coals. You will be burnt! Her motives are evil.

Awake! Shake yourself! It is not innocent. It is a plot with a plan. Dont allow her to put her hooks in you. It doesnt matter that she sought you out. What matters is how you use the principles of wisdom that you were taught.

Remember, the scholar said, Whoever commits adultery, lacks understanding, and destroys his soul. You will destroy yourself, but others will be destroyed also. All of this will occur because you refused to listen to wisdom. You will find yourself looking over your shoulder, because a devastated husband may be seeking revenge. You will be disgraced and the reproach may never go away. There will always be a reminder. Inasmuch as David is known for killing the giant Goliath, he is equally remembered for his adulterous act with Uriahs wife, Bathsheba.

Sneaking and peeking may be private and secret, but it is yelled from the rooftop once you are in their clutches, so beware!

CHAPTER 12

ONLY THE STRONG SURVIVES

LESSON: REACHING THE NEXT GENERATION

My son, keep my words, and lay up my commandments with thee. **Proverbs 7:1**

Retain what you have learned, so you can help someone else. There are those who have not been taught the wisdom you have, so save a life. Help those who cant help themselves. Help those who are being led astray.

Among the youths, there are some silly and simple young men. They are void of understanding. They have not received the training that you have received. When the adulterous women approach them, they will be led away. *Passing through the street near her corner; and he went the way to her house. In the twilight, in the evening, in the black and dark night: And, behold, there met him a woman with the attire of an harlot, and subtle of heart (Proverbs 7:8-10).*

She is in the streets hunting for a precious life. For a period of time she waits at every corner, walking back and forth from corner to corner. She has the patience to wait regardless of the time it takes. Before he knows whats happening, she grabs him and kisses him. She had to conquer him before he could get away. She moves quickly.

After kissing him, she assures him that she came in peace. She emphasizes what she has gone through to prepare for him and find him. *Therefore came I forth to meet thee, diligently to seek thy face, and I have found thee. I have decked my bed with coverings of tapestry, with carved works, with fine linen of Egypt. I have perfumed my bed with myrrh, aloes, and cinnamon. Come, let us take our fill of love until the morning: let us solace ourselves with loves (Proverbs 7:16-18).*

She continued by telling him, her husband was not at home. He was gone on a business trip. Because he took a lot of money with him, she believes his business will take some time. She assures this young man that her husband will not be back for a while, and shell make sure he leaves before her husband returns.

Her speech caused him to feel safe, so he yields. In his weakened state he turns his head from side-to-side, trying to fight the feeling, but she forces him with her lips. He falls, totally surrendering himself to the adulterous woman. When it was over reality hits. He hears the voice of wisdom. Having seen oxen slain, he began to feel like an ox that was led to the slaughter. He felt an unseen dagger piercing through his heart as lifelessness consumed him. ***The innocent has fallen!***

You have been taught wisdom, understanding, and knowledge. It is your responsibility to reach others. Teach them to close their hearts and ears to the voice of the adulteress. Dont go astray following after her. She has wounded many men with her lies and deception. She has destroyed some of the strongest men who ever lived. Her house is the way to hell, and her bedroom is a death sentence.

Tell the young men, that the *men who kept the Law of God on the table of their hearts were the only survivors.*

Survival is escaping, so run for your life!

INDEPENDENT STUDIES

～

Your Independent Studies begin at this juncture of training. Independent Study I, entitled A New Beginning, summarizes Proverbs Chapters 8 through 22. At your own pace, study and meditate on the materials from those chapters. Upon completion, resume your reading with Chapter 14, Opportunity Knocks.

CHAPTER 13

INDEPENDENT STUDY I

LESSON: A NEW BEGINNING

Man oh Man! As I read **Chapters 8 through 22,** I saw an unveiling of Man in his supreme state at various levels. These chapters contain enough valuable information to help every man, woman, and child live a victorious life. However, the immediate audience identified was the man and his son. Wisdom is crying for the attention of man. Men in high places, low places, at the gates, in the cities, and at the doors, anywhere a man can be found. Wisdom cries,

*Unto you, O **men,** I call; and my voice is to the **sons** of man (Proverbs 8:4).*

Even as God is present with you, so is the spirit of wisdom. **There is hidden wealth in wisdom.** Listen to the voice of wisdom and you will hear excellent and right things. Truth and righteousness proceed from the mouth of wisdom. Words of wisdom are plain and easy to understand. Wisdom is better than rubies and all the things that may be compared to it.

Wisdom is creative, enabling you to invent things. Wisdom enables kings to reign and princes to decree justice. Wisdom also equips princes, nobles, and all the judges of the earth to rule. Where you find riches and honor, you will find wisdom. Be alert, the scholar said it is riches with honor and not riches alone. Every man who is rich is not necessarily wise. Wisdom was present with God from the beginning, before He created the heavens and the earth. *Wisdom was established to last forever.* You will be blessed if you keep the ways of wisdom. Whosoever finds wisdom finds life, and shall obtain favor from the Lord.

Throughout these chapters, men of various characteristics were discussed in the light of wisdom. The seven character types included: a *wise* man, a *righteous* man, a *faithful* man, a *prudent* man, a *merciful* man, a *just* man, and a *good* man.

This independent study session will prove most beneficial on a personal level. Using the information contained in chapters eight through twenty-two, you are encouraged to examine yourself and make decisions and changes needful for your life. You have been taught, now you must teach others. These chapters do not contain any surprises. They simply reinforce what you have already been taught. If the teachings have resinated within you, you can now further develop yourself and teach others.

You are equipped to answer pointed questions about yourself.

Who are you?

What is your true identity?

Will your character sustain a victorious life?

What will you become?

What decisions do you need to make?

What decisions will you actually make?

It is evident that God deeply cares about man, not just generally as mankind, but also gender specific. The instructions included are priceless. Every man can visualize, decide, and become the type of man he aspires to. Turn the page and study these attributes, memorize them, and make them a part of your life.

LETS BEGIN AT THE BEGINNING ~ YOU

GOD and MAN

➢ Every wise mans blessing is wrapped up in his ability to walk in wisdom daily.

➢ Every way of a man is right in his own eyes, but the Lord ponders the heart.

➢ A mans heart devises his way, but the Lord directs his steps.

➢ When a mans ways please the Lord, his enemies will be at peace with him.

➢ A mans gift makes room for him and brings him before great men.

➢ Mans goings are of the Lord; how can a man then understand his own way?

➢ A mans belly shall be satisfied with the fruit of his mouth.

➢ There is a way that seems right unto a man, but at the end are the ways of death.

➢ The way of man is froward and strange, but as for the pure, his work is right.

➢ A mans pride shall bring him low, but honor shall uphold the humble in spirit.

➢ All the ways of a man are clean in his own eyes, but the Lord weighs the spirits.

➢ The preparations of mans heart and the answer of his tongue are from the Lord.

➢ The words of a mans mouth are as deep waters and wisdom as a flowing brook.

➢ *The spirit of man is a candle of the Lord, searching the inward parts of the belly.*

➢ The spirit of a man will sustain his infirmity, but a wounded spirit who can bear?

- It is an honor for a man to cease from strife, but every fool will be meddling.
- It is a snare to the man, who devours that which is holy and questions his vows.
- The man who departs from understanding shall be aimlessly lost.
- Dont befriend an angry man and dont go anywhere with a furious man.

A HEART of WISDOM

- A wise man controls his anger.
- A wise man is strong.
- *A wise man increases his strength with more knowledge.*
- A wise man fears and departs from evil.
- Rebuke a wise man and he will love thee.
- A wise man controls his tongue and does not speak all of his mind.
- A wise man defeats the mighty and casts down the strong.
- A wise man destroys his rest when he debates with a fool.

The FAVOUR of GOD

- A wise man obtains favor of the Lord.
- *He that diligently seeks good procures favour.*
- Good understanding yields favor.
- Among the righteous there is favor.
- Loving favour is preferred over loving silver and gold.
- A rebuke brings more favour than a flattering tongue.
- The kings favour is as dew upon the grass.
- You can have favour with God and man.

The *WISE NEEDS COUNSELING*

- Give instruction to a wise man and he will be yet wiser.
- There are many *devices* in a mans heart.
- Without counsel *purposes* are disappointed.
- Where there is no counsel the *people* fall.
- The counsel of the Lord shall stand forever.
- Sound wisdom and great understanding produce *good counsel.*
- *Hear* counsel and *receive* instruction that you may be wise in the end.
- **In the multitude of counselors, there is safety, and purposes are established.**
- Every purpose is established, by counsel and good advice.
- The sweetness of a friends hearty counsel rejoices the heart.
- He who listens to counsel is wise.
- Counsel in the heart is like deep water, but understanding will draw it out.
- There is no wisdom, nor understanding, nor counsel *against the Lord.*

DILIGENCE WILL PROMOTE YOU

- The hand of the diligent becomes rich.
- The hand of the diligent shall rule.
- The soul of the diligent shall be made fat.
- The thoughts of the diligent produce abundance.
- The substance of a diligent man is precious.
- Be diligent to know the state of your affairs.
- **See thou a man diligent in his business? He shall stand before kings!**

LAZINESS IS NOT AN OPTION

➤ *Laziness turns into lifelessness.*

➤ The slothful man does not roast that, which he caught in hunting; its too much work. He has no *motivation!*

➤ The way of the slothful man is as a hedge of thorns everything is too hard. *He is not innovative or creative!*

➤ A slothful man hides his hand in his bosom and will not so much as bring it to his mouth again. *He has no hope!*

➤ The slothful man says, There is a lion outside, I shall be slain in the streets. Any excuse works for a lazy man. *He will not prosper!*

➤ There is an end to every man and for the lazy man there is no difference. Drowsiness shall clothe a man with rags!

BENEFITS of LIVING RIGHT

➤ The mouth of a righteous man is a well of life.

➤ The labour of the righteous, nurtures to life.

➤ The fruit of the righteous is a tree of life.

➤ The righteous shall flourish as a branch.

➤ The righteous is an everlasting foundation.

➤ The righteous are bold as a lion.

➤ The thoughts of the righteous are right.

➤ A righteous man hates lying.

➤ Kings love him who speaks what is right.

➤ The lips of the righteous feed many.

➤ The righteous gives and spares not.

➤ The righteous considers the cause of the poor.

➤ The heart of the righteous, studies to answer.

➤ The righteous good shall be re-payed.

➤ The lips of the righteous know what is acceptable.

➤ The Lord will not suffer the soul of the righteous to famish.

- ➤ The desire of the righteous is only good.
- ➤ The righteous runs to the Lord and is safe.
- ➤ The Lord hears the prayer of the righteous.
- ➤ The desire of the righteous shall be granted.
- ➤ The seed of the righteous shall be delivered.
- ➤ The hope of the righteous shall be gladness.
- ➤ The way of the righteous is made plain.
- ➤ The righteous shall never be removed.
- ➤ The father of the righteous shall greatly rejoice.
- ➤ When righteous men rejoice there is great glory.
- ➤ The root of the righteous shall not be moved.
- ➤ The root of the righteous yields fruit.
- ➤ In the house of the righteous is much treasure.
- ➤ The house of the righteous shall stand.
- ➤ The light of the righteous rejoices.
- ➤ The righteous is delivered out of trouble.
- ➤ A righteous man regards the life of his beast.
- ➤ The righteous is more excellent than his neighbor.
- ➤ The righteous sings and rejoices.
- ➤ ***When the righteous are in authority, the people rejoice.***
- ➤ When it goes well with the righteous, the city rejoices.
- ➤ It is not good to overthrow the righteous in judgment.
- ➤ The righteous shall be recompensed in the earth.
- ➤ The righteous eats to the satisfying of his soul.
- ➤ With the righteous there is favor.
- ➤ The righteous hath hope even in his death.

FAITHFULNESS IS CRITICAL

- ➤ A faithful man shall abound with blessings.
- ➤ He who has a faithful spirit conceals a secret.
- ➤ A faithful ambassador is health to himself and others.

- A faithful witness will not lie.
- *Faithful are the wounds of a friend.*
- A faithful messenger refreshes the soul of his leader.

FORESIGHT of the PRUDENT

- The prudent man is crowned with knowledge.
- The wise in heart shall be called prudent.
- *The wisdom of the prudent is to understand his way.*
- The prudent man looks deep into his going.
- The heart of the prudent gets knowledge.
- Every prudent man conceals his knowledge.
- Every prudent man deals with knowledge.
- A prudent man covers shame.
- A prudent man endures reproof.
- A prudent man foresees evil and hides himself.

FORGIVING YOURSELF

- The *merciful man* does good to his own soul.

JUSTICE PREVAILS

- Teach a *just man* and he will increase in learning.
- The *just man* walks in his integrity.
- *A just man falls seven times and rises up again.*

IT PAYS to do GOOD

- A *good man* obtains favor of the Lord.
- A *good man* leaves an inheritance to his childrens children.
- A *good man* shall be satisfied with himself.

GOING BEYOND YOURSELF ~ OTHERS

Wise, righteous, faithful, prudent, merciful, just, and good men multiply! ***The works of their character extend beyond themselves.***

A WISE SON

A wise son hears his fathers instructions.
He that gathers in summer is a wise son.
A wise son makes a glad father.
The father who loves his son chastises him when necessary.

Your LEGACY

In order for the children to hear and hearken to the instructions of a father, you must teach them by precept and example. Their blessings rest on their commitment to retain and obey what they have been taught.

- ೋ Hell and destruction are before the Lord: how much more then the hearts of the children of men?
- ೋ In the fear of the Lord is strong confidence: and his children shall have a place of refuge.
- ೋ Childrens children are the crown of old men; and the glory of children are their fathers.
- ೋ ***The just man walks in his integrity: his children are blessed after him.***
- ೋ A good man leaves an inheritance to his childrens children: and the wealth of the sinner is laid up for the just.

The PROVERBS 31 WOMAN

- ∞ Every *wise* woman builds her house.
- ∞ A *gracious* woman retains honor.
- ∞ A *virtuous* woman is a crown to her husband.

The OTHER WOMAN

- ∞ A *foolish* woman is clamorous, simple, and knows nothing.
- ∞ A *fair* woman without discretion is like gold in a pigs snout.
- ∞ It is better to dwell in the wilderness, than with a *contentious* and *angry* woman.
- ∞ It is better to dwell in a corner of the housetop, than with a *brawling* woman in a wide house.

Let the words of my mouth, and the meditations of my heart, be acceptable in thy sight, O Lord, my strength, and my redeemer (Psalm 19:14).

CHAPTER 14

OPPORTUNITY KNOCKS

LESSON: ETHICS

My son, if thine heart be wise, my heart shall rejoice, even mine.
Proverbs 23:15

Before the training began a foundation was laid, Maintaining your character when opportunity knocks.

Everyone is governed by moral principles. However, the degree of morality may differ from group to group. Nevertheless, it is the human character that separates the rights and the wrongs for each group.

You are wise enough to know that every open door is not an opportunity, so dont get tricked or trapped. Even a seat among the rich and famous must be viewed cautiously. Dont foolishly rush in and make yourself comfortable. Motives are premium! Tread lightly and walk softly. Dont be envious of others riches. Riches are not the fulfillment of life. Like life, however, riches are here today and can be gone tomorrow.

Man is the product of whats in his heart! All of the issues of life can be addressed from your heart. All of the character-building training you have received, and the wisdom you have been given should be your measuring stick. It is critical that you do not remove the landmarks of your life. These landmarks are your *Memorials of Truth*. They serve as a reminder to you and your legacy. The scholar says, It is good to correct your actions, but dont forget to correct your children also. It is your responsibility and you will be held accountable. Correcting your children can deliver them from the wrong path.

In this training, the scholar says, My son, if thine heart be wise, my heart shall rejoice, even mine. I easily related to the scholar. I used to believe that I possessed an abundance of wisdom in my heart, until I saw wisdom in my daughter. When I see the wisdom of my daughter, my legacy, it makes me smile and my heart rejoices, just as the scholar stated.

The scholar is attempting to build you up and encourage you to remember the rewards of wisdom. He said,

! When you are wise your speech is with wisdom.
! When you are wise you reverence God.
! When you are wise your expectations will not be cut off.

You must guide your heart. You must not faint. Stay focused and never detour from truth.

There are enemies, distractors, and destroyers of wisdom. The scholar warns you to stay away from them. Separate yourself from the winebibbers, drunkards, rioters, and even the ones controlled by gluttony. Extreme is not the limit for these vices. They will ultimately lead you to poverty.

This is the last item for this session; nevertheless, it is critical to your walk of wisdom. To ignore this is to fail. This warning is unlike the previous warnings, yet it can be the difference between life and death. It is: Even when your father and mother are old, listen to them, because they possess an advanced level of wisdom. *Someone once said, Listening is a sign of strength, not weakness. We learn when we listen to what others have to say.*

CHAPTER 15

FALSE SATISFACTION

---◦◦◦◦◦◦---

LESSON: THE WHORE AND WINE

My son, give me thine heart, and let thine eyes observe my ways.
Proverbs 23:26

When you become the man who can boldly ask your son to give you his heart, and to watch the life you live, you are becoming the Proverbs 31 Man. However, when he gives you his heart, you must consistently be the example that he can follow, and the role model that he desires to emulate. The need to search for a role model should be non-existent for him.

Wisdom in your heart helps to keep your eyes and ears alert. You must even be observant of your surroundings at all times. Be conscious of what is happening around your son. Observe the wandering eyes and the talking with their hands. Dont be caught unaware. You have been warned about the strange and adulterous women, but listen to the description of the *whore*. A whore is a **deep ditch!**

Just because you resisted the strange woman dont get too confident. You must always be alert. The plots, plans, and strategies are different at every level. The strange woman was a **narrow pit** compared to the whore, who is a deep ditch. If you fall in, you may not be able to dig yourself out. She is on the prowl like the adulterous woman, but she is not looking for a precious life to ruin, she is looking for a *prey.* She is hunting you

62

to kill you. She will eat you alive and spit you out. Her reputation is well-known. She is accredited with increasing the number of fallen men. Yet, she portrays herself as the antidote for all the issues of man. She promises to wipe away their regrets, sadness, and heartaches.

Her clientele is vast. She advertises to all men and she covers all bases. She specifically identifies six circumstances, which a man might experience. Ironically, all of the areas she addresses are emotional. You probably were taught as I was, to separate yourself from your emotions when making decisions. Yet, her pursuit is directed to the emotions of every man, single and married. *Who hath woe? Who hath sorrow? Who hath contentions? Who hath babbling? Who hath wounds without cause? Who hath redness of eyes? (Proverbs 23:29)*

She invites the men who have woes, great sorrows. This can be in general or living with a wife. Then she calls those who are just sad or disappointed with their lives. She sends a shout out to those who find themselves constantly in the midst of heated arguments and hostile disagreements. To all she says, Come!

Knowing and understanding the nature of man, she didnt dare leave out the men, who were tired of listening to the non-stop murmurings and complaints. She extended a special invitation to men who were dealing with wounds from being wronged and treated unjustly. Her invitation also goes to the man who is experiencing sleepless nights, as revealed in his red eyes. However, she doesnt stop there. She invites the drunk. His eyes are red and he is hung over. She assures him that if he is not welcomed anywhere else, she welcomes him. This womans invitation reaches across all boundaries.

You already know that wine dulls your senses, impairs your judgment, and reduces your self-control, but know for certain, the whore will do far more damage to you than the wine.

It is stated, Wine bites like a *large* snake and stings like a *poisonous* snake. Likewise, when the whore bites, you become numb and confused. You are like a zombie. You are putty in her hands.

When you entangle yourself with the whore, perverse things will come out of your heart; things you didnt even know were in your heart. You will become helpless against her. You will be as one lying in the midst of the sea with no help in sight. Before you know it, you will be saying: *They have stricken me, and I was not sick; they have beaten me, and I felt it not: when shall I awake? I will seek it **yet again*** (Proverbs 23:35).

Hooked and Hopeless!

CHAPTER 16

CUTTING OFF

————————⟨⟩————————

LESSON: ENVY OR EXPECTATION

My son, eat thou honey, because it is good; and the honeycomb,
which is sweet to thy taste: So shall the knowledge of wisdom
be unto thy soul: when thou hast found it, then there shall be a
reward, and thy expectation shall not be cut off.
Proverbs 24:13-14

Envy is one of the most dangerous emotions in the heart of
man. It is called the *green-eyed monster.* Youve probably heard
the phrase, *Green with Envy*; thus, you are not aware of a persons
envy until it reveals its ugly head. It is a secret emotion. The
dangers of envy trump even the emotion of hatred. Right, wrong,
or indifferent, there is an inner reason why you hate. Your hatred
is not usually a secret and you will tell anyone who listens or
thinks like you. Not Envy!

The attributes of envy reside in the dark cold area of an
unwise heart. These attributes will remain hidden until the
discontentment of life, *exceeds* the will to do what is right.

You can recognize when the green-eyed monster is forming.
It starts when you no longer see people; instead, you see what
they possess. Then you start evaluating what you have and dont
have. The results are deadly. You begin to long after others
possessions, desiring them for yourself. You believe they have

what you should have. Then a transformation occurs in your heart, you secretly switch places with them.

Envy, *in the simplest term,* is cruel and destructive. It can destroy the hunter and the prey. Before presenting his next lesson, Solomon warns you about envying evil men. You must remember, even when you are aware of their evil doings, your eyes see their prosperity. It no longer seems to matter that they are promoting gangs, guns, prostitution, drugs, or even human trafficking. You see their possessions. You are cautioned not to envy them or desire to be with them.

The scholar switches his attention to the wise man. He encourages him. He reminds the wise man that he is strong. However, if he faints and doesnt make the right decision his strength is small, and he will not withstand the test. The wise man must use what he knows about evil men to fortify himself. He must observe and learn; thereby, strengthening himself to say, No, to the temptations.

The more knowledge a man obtains, the more strength he possesses. A wise man will not be influenced by foolishness. *He builds his house in wisdom, establishes it with understanding, and uses his knowledge to fill it.*

After an intense lesson on envy, Solomon leaves that bitter issue and makes a transition to the sweet. His symbolic example of wisdom was eating honey and the honeycomb. Its sweet! He reminds his son that the knowledge of wisdom is sweetness to his mind. Wisdom does not create confusion in your mind like envy.

One of his most profound key points was, When you possess wisdom, your expectation will not be cut off! Oh, if you could only see the countless expectations, which died and were left by the side of the road. Someone said, The cemetery is filled with unfulfilled expectations and dreams. Nevertheless,

Solomon reminds his son, Even if you fall seven times and your expectation seemingly is cut off, dont despair, but rise up again. After you are back on your feet and you are stabilized, strengthen your brother. Dont dare rejoice when your enemy stumbles or falls. This will displease the Lord. You have been reminded repeatedly, dont fret over evil men neither be envious of wicked men. Your end is so much brighter than theirs!

CHAPTER 17

THINKING OF YOU

LESSON: JUST A REMINDER

My son, fear thou the Lord and the king: and meddle not with them that are given to change: For their calamity shall rise suddenly; and who knoweth the ruin of them both?
Proverbs 24:21-22

You have been taught the characteristics of a wise man. Listen and aspire to walk in wisdom. These are some of the ways of the wise. You

- dont have respect of persons, in judgment,
- dont call the wicked, righteous,
- support the person who answers in truth,
- prepare for work,
- prioritize your home and business,
- are not a false witness,
- are not deceptive,
- dont seek revenge, and,
- pay every man according to his work.

If you compare a wise man to a slothful man and a man who does not have good understanding, you will clearly see the prosperity of wisdom.

In the remaining verses, Solomon gives an illustration:

*I went by the field of the slothful, and by the vineyard of the man void of understanding; And, lo, it was all **grown over** with thorns, and nettles had **covered** the face thereof, and the stone wall thereof was **broken down.** Then I saw, and considered it well: I looked upon it, and received instructions. Yet a little sleep, a little slumber, a little folding of the hands to sleep: So shall thy poverty come as one that travels; and thy want as an armed man. (Proverbs 24:30-34)*

Remember who you are and do what you were trained to do.

INDEPENDENT STUDIES

≈

Your Independent Study II, Leaders, begins here. It includes summaries of Proverbs Chapters 25 and 26. At your own pace, study and meditate on the materials from those chapters. Upon completion, resume your reading with Chapter 19, Its Up To You.

CHAPTER 18

INDEPENDENT STUDY II

LESSON: LEADERS

Proverbs **Chapters 25 and 26** contain a massive amount of instructions. The scholar directs his attention to every man, who aspires to be a leader. The first truth is, Every wise man is not a leader. You were all designed to lead in some aspects or another. However, you were not all designed to fill the office of a Leader. Be sure that there is a Leader in you. A false leader is like clouds and wind, without rain. A false leader cannot meet the expectations of a leader. People will be looking for something that will never happen.

This session is designed to nurture the leader in you. Absorb it at your own pace. Identify the areas in your life that needs to be developed, in order for you to become a leader. Whatever you do, do it with all your heart. Know assuredly, that there will be many demands on you as a leader. You are cautioned not to seek leadership, because you think it looks good.

The result of wise leadership is that it brings glory to God. Gods eyes go back and forth in all the earth looking at the good and the evil. When you are a leader, he reveals things to you if he deems it necessary. However, as a leader, you should discern and investigate things that are contrary to your leadership.

Your first method of investigation should be prayer. The wise leader investigates a matter to unveil the things, which were done in the dark. Works of darkness undermine good leadership.

Therefore, remove wickedness from under your leadership and righteousness will prevail.

When there is a leader in you, you dont have to force it. You dont have to pretentiously come into the presence of other leaders; or stand nearby that you may be seen. Wait for an invitation to join them, and you wont be embarrassed if they ask you to move. Be yourself, and the things you have to offer will open doors for you.

The leader, who is consistently ready for a good debate, loses sight of the difficulties it creates in communication. It is also critical that a leader knows how to maintain the privacy of others. Any concerns should be discussed directly with the person involved and in private. Open controversies open the door to dissension and division. You must use all of your insight into each situation, and settle the matter wisely. Information shared with you in secret should not be shared with others. You must respect the privacy of those who confide in you.

Your greatest influence with people is a kind word. Someone said, Kind words are like golden ripe apples in a shiny silver basket. And you have been taught that a soft answer can diffuse anger and change the atmosphere. You may be the leader, but its the people around you that determine the degree of influence you will have. When you have faithful supporters, you can be confident that they will cover your back. However, dont use your position as an opportunity to abuse them. You must respect the relationship and give it room to grow. Dont interfere in their life being nosy and trying to find out things they didnt voluntarily share.

As a wise leader, you cannot allow others to persuade you to go against your character. However, you must treat everyone with equity and integrity--even your enemy. You must be willing to go the extra mile.

The scholar makes a sudden and strategic turn from your leadership ability with others, to specifically discuss your leadership ability with your wife, a woman. In addition, this example is of an unwise woman. She fights so much that a big house cant shield you. You escape to the rooftop and she follows you there.

Nevertheless, the wise leader must deal with this unwise woman with as much kindness as you dealt with the angry uncompromising associates. You must remember that the same influence works with her, a kind word. Your response to her could possibly influence her to change for the better. She is not to be regarded with less compassion and patience than that, which was done outside of the home. If there is a wise leader within you, an unwise woman could surely be the tester, which brings it to the surface.

Finally, you reach the end of your probation period and realize, you have passed all the tests of a wise leader. You cant help but feel good. The feeling of satisfaction brings a smile to your lips. Be careful and walk softly! The wise leader whose actions have resulted in a good outcome must not seek glory for it. To seek your own glory is not glory at all. It is vanity! Let your works praise you. Allow others to encourage you. Do not parade around like a peacock thinking you have arrived and should be crowned. Take control of yourself. Dont go off the deep end. A leader who does not control his spirit is like a city that is broken down, and has no walls. There is no protection from the onslaughts!

The instructions contained in **Chapter 26** are thought-provoking for the wise leader. The scholar shows what a wise leader is not! He lists the contrasting characteristics of a fool, a slothful man, and a talebearer. Just as darkness departs when light is turned on, these three characteristics should never be a part of a wise leaders persona.

About the **fool,** the scholar says,

- ൪ do not give them honor,
- ൪ do not respond to the stupidity of a fool,
- ൪ do not send a message by a fool,
- ൪ do not listen to a proverb quoted by fools,
- ൪ do not place a fool in a position of authority, and,
- ൪ do not hire a fool or a drunk.

About the **slothful,** the scholar says,

- ൪ they will find every excuse not to move,
- ൪ they will imagine things that dont exist,
- ൪ they will turn over in their warm beds,
- ൪ they will pull the covers over their heads,
- ൪ they are too lazy to lift a fork to their mouths, and,
- ൪ they are dreamers who fantasize their self-worth.

About the **talebearer,** the scholar says,

- ൪ they are like chameleons, they change with each situation,
- ൪ they meddle in things thats none of their business,
- ൪ they are deliberately deceptive and argumentative,
- ൪ they say things kiddingly that they really mean,
- ൪ they are the source of most arguments, and,
- ൪ they keep the gossip alive so the fighting will continue.

The scholar summarizes, You may not be a fool, a slothful man, or a talebearer, but you must be on the alert for them. They will approach you and you must be ready.

Since the talebearer is the one who changes with each situation, the scholar provides further warnings regarding the talebearer.

- ⚘ Listening to gossip is like putting spoiled foods into your belly.
- ⚘ Listening to smooth talk from a deceptive person is like a knife in the heart.
- ⚘ Greeting an enemy like a friend is like placing a serpent in your bosom.
- ⚘ Shaking hands with a conniver is like sleeping with the enemy.
- ⚘ Accepting the words of a deceiver is like giving your house key to a robber.
- ⚘ Responding to flattery from a talebearer will bring you to ruin.

LEADERSHIP IS NOT ONLY A ROLE,
IT IS A RESPONSIBILITY!

CHAPTER 19

ITS UP TO YOU

LESSON: A SURVIVING LEGACY

My son, be wise, and make my heart glad,
that I may answer him that reproacheth me.
Proverbs 27:11

The beginning of this session continues with the Leadership theme from the Independent Study. It is understood that every wise leader must plan. However, you must not become boastful and think you are calling the shots.

At the beginning of this training you were reminded that God is your foundation. He is in control. You are here today, but tomorrow is not promised to you. You have no idea what tomorrow may bring, so let humility reign in your heart. The scholar repeats the warning, Allow others to praise you. Dont elevate yourself. It will stir up anger and jealousy.

You are encouraged to diligently retain wisdom in your heart, to prevent the evil things from entering. And wisdom will teach you to discern and recognize evil things. Wrath is cruel and anger is outrageous; but who is able to stand before envy? Open rebuke is better than secret love. Faithful are the wounds of a friend; but the kisses of an enemy are deceitful (Proverbs 27:4-6).

After the warnings and encouragement, his attention is redirected to the son, his future, and his *Legacy.* A plea is made for the son to be wise and make his dad happy. This will enable the dad to answer those who try to discredit his son. However, the son must avoid disgraceful behaviors. He must use his insight, his teachings, and discernment, to foresee evil and avoid it at all cost.

The instructions regarding friends must have been important because the scholar readdresses the influences of friends. Friendships will influence and strengthen you to do or not to do. It is stated, Iron sharpens iron, and a man sharpens the countenance of his friend.It is evident that friends are important. However, your friends should compliment you and what you represent.

Friendship joins the heart of one individual to that of another. You must be diligent to know the hearts of those who surround you. Dont be misled by riches, because they do not last forever. Another reality is, even that which you desire for your *Legacy* may not continue through every generation.

Keep moving forward and dont give up. A remnant of a Legacy is better than no Legacy at all.

INDEPENDENT STUDIES

～

Your Independent Study III, Leadership, begins here. It includes summaries of Proverbs Chapters 28 through 30. At your own pace, study and meditate on the materials from those chapters. Upon completion, resume your reading with Chapter 21, the final chapter, titled, The Proverbs 31 Man and His Woman!

CHAPTER 20

INDEPENDENT STUDY III

LESSON: LEADERSHIP

These last three chapters, **Proverbs Chapters 28 through 30,** are filled with contrasts for you to remember. Although your teachings have covered all of these areas, the scholar deemed it necessary to repeat them in a different way. There are no examples, just plain and simple contrasts of the wise leader to the wicked, evil, and poor leaders. However, only the positive reinforcements are captured in this study to ensure that your heart is strengthened and encouraged to move forward from here, to you know where.

From **Chapter 28,** we have captured 10 Commandments for the wise Leader.

10 COMMANDMENTS for LEADERS

I. Thou shall be bold as a lion.

II. Thou shall be a man of understanding and knowledge.

III. Thou shall keep the Law of God.

IV. Thou shall show compassion to the poor.

V. Thou shall pray with a clean heart.

VI. Thou shall rejoice and give God glory.

VII. Thou shall confess and forsake sin.

VIII. Thou shall reverence God and maintain a tender heart.

IX. Thou shall be faithful and abound in blessings.

X. Thou shall put your trust in God.

Even though we are approaching the end of the instructions, there is a sudden sense of urgency, in **Chapter 29.** The scholar has taught the same lessons over and over, in different formats and settings. At this point, he needs to know your heart has received what was given to you. Now, he reinforces the *consequences.* If you refuse to abide by the Laws of God, you will be destroyed without remedy. No hope of recovery!

Although you have decided to be a wise leader, you still need to be reminded about the ugly side of bad leadership. If you keep the 10 Commandments for Leaders, you will be a wise leader; yet, if you choose not to, there are 20 Consequences of Bad Leadership waiting for you.

20 CONSEQUENCES of BAD LEADERSHIP

I. When a leader is bad, everyone suffers.
II. When a leader keeps company with a prostitute, he spends all his money.
III. When a leader is influenced with bribes, he becomes indifferent.
IV. When a leader sets a trap for others, he will fall in his own trap.
V. When a leader is hardhearted, he cares nothing about the poor.
VI. When a leader allows gangs to run freely, everybody lives in fear.
VII. When a leader allows murderers to attack honest people, he is a reproach.
VIII. When a leader is angry and says everything that is on his mind, he is a fool.
IX. When a leader listens to malicious gossip, he infects those around him.

X. When a leader fails to discipline his children, they will embarrass him.

XI. When a leader is bad and appoints bad leaders, crime increases.

XII. When a leader has no vision, the economy crashes.

XIII. When a leader is bad, the people ignore whatever they say.

XIV. When a leader doesnt think before he speaks, he is headed for ruin.

XV. When a leader is angry and stirs up trouble, everyone is miserable.

XVI. When a leaders pride is out of control, he will fall flat on his face.

XVII. When a leader joins forces with a thief, he is his own worst enemy.

XVIII. When a leader lives in fear, he is destined for failure.

XIX. When a leader thinks he owns those following him, unreasonable demands increase.

XX. When a leader is unjust, he cant stand the sight of the just.

This session, **Chapter 30,** the chapter preceding the chapter on which the foundation of this training manual rests. It brings us to the door where the fullness of man should be shining as the sun. Yet, the chapter begins with a man proclaiming his insensitivity, his lack of understanding of *man,* and the absence of wisdom and the knowledge of God.

What? Is he a man or a beast? At this point of the training, every aspect of life has been addressed and covered extensively. Is it possible that some of you will reach this point, and still not accept what it is to be a wise man? Just because it is possible, it doesnt have to be YOU.

During his outburst, the man discharges several challenging questions, one after the other. He has already confessed that he does not know; but now he wants to know do you, the wise man, know. All of his questions pertain to God. This reinforces the lesson that every wise mans foundation is God!

In the midst of what looks like hopelessness, a wise man speaks up. You can clearly see that he is applying his training. With few words he answered the foolish man. He said, Every word of God is true. He protects everyone who trusts Him. Dont challenge Him because He will put you to shame.

After witnessing the actions of the foolish man, the wise man became overwhelmed. The thought of him becoming like this man caused him to redirect his attention to God. He prayed, God, Im asking for two things before I die. Please dont refuse me. First, remove vanity and lies from my heart. Secondly, dont allow me to be poor or rich, but give me enough food to live on. Dont give me too much, because I might get independent and say I dont need you. Dont give me too little, because I might steal from others and dishonor your name.

The scholar resumes his leadership lesson. This is his final opportunity to make an impact, so the sessions are strong and they are many. The first lesson is directed to you, as a leader. You are encouraged to never back-stab anyone. Being underhanded is not a trait for wise leaders. Do not demean yourself in the eyes of those you are appointed to lead. And always consider the generation you are leading.

GENERATION after GENERATION

Some experts say, that the standard number of generations in a century is four, however, it can go up to five, with childbirths and life-spans being the reasons for the increase.

We have the characteristics of four generations listed here:

! There is a generation that curses their father, and fails to bless their mother. The fifth commandment of the Law of God (Honor your mother and father) means nothing to them.

! There is a generation that believes beauty is in the eyes of the beholder, because in their eyes they are pure, even when their hearts are filthy.

! There is a generation that walks around with their head in the cloud and nose in the air thinking they are better than everyone else.

! There is a generation that cares about nothing or no one. They will eat you alive and not give it a thought. They show no mercy. Their teeth are like a sword that pierces and a knife that cuts. They devour the poor and the needy.

IT IS NOT ENOUGH

Greed is a mental substance abuse. Nothing will *ever* be enough; and Everything will *never* be enough! From your beginning to your ending, ever and never rule!

Greed is compared to four things, which are never satisfied; hell, a barren womb, a parched land, and a forest fire. These will take and take, but will never say, It Is Enough!

In-between sessions, the scholar slides in another reminder to honor your mother and father that the days of your life may be lengthened.

UNDERSTANDING LIFE

In this session, the scholar shares his amazement of seeing and understanding the normal course of life in three things, but the fourth thing astonishes him.

He marvels at:

~how an eagle flies so high in the sky and never loses its way;
~how a snake glides over a rock whether it is smooth or
   rough; and,
~how a ship is navigated in the ocean and not get swallowed
   by its vastness.

However, the way of a man with a maid baffles him. He gives an example. The prostitute has sex with her client. She gets up, takes a bath, rises up, and says, I am innocent. Its not surprising he would be baffled. I believe this would baffle the greatest intellect.

During my lifetime I have heard it repeated so many times, You cant figure a woman out; just when you think you understand her, she changes. Rather than this being a joke followed by laughter, the main lesson here is: If you have a Proverbs 31 Woman, dont try to figure her out or place her in a box, just be the Proverbs 31 Man that compliments her and all she represents!

LIFEs CHALLENGES

There are things, events, and acts that shake the very foundation of life. Some are controllable and others are not. This session illustrates three things, which are troubling for you as a leader:

~the servant who becomes the boss,
~a fool who becomes rich, and,
~a nasty married woman.

However, the fourth thing is so devastating that no one should have to endure it, a girlfriend replacing a faithful wife.

LIFEs MOTIVATION

There are four small creatures upon the earth, but they are listed among the wisest of the wise.

! The *ants* are frail, yet they store plenty of food in the summer, so they will be able to eat in the winter.

! The *conies* are feeble rodents, and as vulnerable as they are, they manage to build rock-solid homes.

! The *locusts* are grasshoppers without a leader, yet they unite together like an army and strip the fields.

! The *spiders* are easy to catch, but they sneak past everyone who would stop them and get into the kings palace and build their homes.

LEADERSHIP

There is a leader in you. You must decide what type. The scholar mentions four leadership types, which one describes you?

!   A lion which is strongest among beasts and turneth not away for any; and,

!   A greyhound; an he goat also; and a king against whom there is no rising up.

There was a lot of information in **Chapter 30**, yet it ends with a warning. Dont let your emotions get the best of you. If you bring attention to yourself by offending people and making rude gestures, dont be surprised if someone bloodies your nose. Remember, riled up emotions can turn into fistfights or gun killings!

CHAPTER 21

PROVERBS 31

LESSON: THE PROVERBS 31 MAN and HIS WOMAN

WOW! We have finally reached the lead-in of the main storyline: Proverbs 31:1-9. Here is a King, a son who is proud to share what his mother taught him. He even refers to himself the way his mother referred to him, i.e., my son, the son of my womb, and the son of my vows. She warns him about women and wine. She reminds him of his destiny and his purpose, as a king and a man.

Then, she gives him the *template* of the wife he must find (Proverbs 31:10-31).

THE PROVERBS 31 MAN
10. Who can find a virtuous woman? for her price is far above rubies.

The man is the *Who* in this passage. When he answers the question, he says, I am he because he recognizes that he is a Proverbs 31 Man. He is a godly man, a visionary, and a man of integrity and commitment. He is a virtuous man. He is a man of character, looking for a woman of character.

Since the *Who* comes before the *What*, it implies that there is a requirement first for the man, before he finds the *What*, a virtuous woman. To find this woman of character, whose virtue is seen in her lifestyle, this man must have something to offer. He is a king, but not necessarily in the office of an earthly king.

His life is such, that it generates the accolades of a king; and this royal man wants to find a royal wife. He is a king of a man, who is seeking to find a queen of a woman. She will become the crown that he wears (Proverbs 12:4). A virtuous woman is a **crown** to her husband.

Its no coincidence that the chapter starts with King Lemuel reciting what his mother taught him, and the warnings she had given him. By the time you reach the tenth verse, your heart and mind should envision *nothing less* than a king, the **Proverbs 31 Man.** Gods Word declares that you have been made kings and priests in His sight.

A good man, who is walking in obedience to God, obtains favour from the Lord continually (Proverbs 12:2). With or without the *What*, the virtuous woman, this man is continually walking in the favour of God.

The blessedness of his obedience decreases his chances of making mistakes, wrong decisions, and bad choices, because God is directing his footsteps (Psalm 37:23).

When this virtuous man goes looking for his virtuous woman, having his steps directed, he will not select the wrong person based on the wrong reasons. Marriage is a much easier process, when both the King and Queen are married to the one God intended. The Spirit of God will lead and guide the man to the right woman. God will even give him a confirmation that she is the right woman.

The only way this man can walk in obedience to God is to know the Word of God. And because he knows the Word of God, he knows virtue. The Word taught him virtue. He also knows what the Word says about the deceitful woman and the vanity of her beauty. His eyes are enlightened and he cannot be tricked easily.

In following Gods instructions, The Proverbs 31 Man finds his virtuous woman. When he finds her, he realizes that she is more valuable than he thought. He learns first-hand that *her price is truly far above rubies.* He becomes awe struck when he discovers that because of her, he is getting *more* favour from the Lord. (Proverbs 18:22) He was already blessed with favour as a good man, and now having found his wife, his favour just increased; with a different kind of favour.

There are different levels and types of favour. For example,

- ✠ I need you to do me a favor, lend me $250.00.
- ✠ I need you to do me a favor, let me borrow your car.
- ✠ I need you to do me a favor, my family is coming to town and they need somewhere to stay for a week. Can they stay with you?

This visionary realizes that if he lives a life of integrity and commits to the sanctity of marriage, the continual favour of God *increases.* It is a *win-win* situation! This reveals the wisdom of the Proverbs 31 Man. We cannot overlook the fact that he is a man of faith. Just as it takes faith to commit your life and will to God, it takes faith to commit your life and will to a wife.

This lesson really needs to be taught to our single young men and women. Because the truth is, the characteristics of a virtuous man and a virtuous woman have to be developed long before marriage. There is no dowry that can contain what the Word of God teaches, or where the Holy Spirit leads.

For those already married, your focus should not be on the weaknesses of your spouse. Rather, you should seek to understand what the Bible says about your marriage. Then, with all diligence apply the principles of Gods Word to your marriage. This can result in you enjoying the type of marriage that God promised.

God invests in marriages by blessing you and causing you to become a blessing. Therefore, your marriage should glorify God.

AND HIS WOMAN
10. Who can find a virtuous woman? for her price is far above rubies.

I believe King Xerxes and others would agree that Esther was a virtuous woman. Her name meant righteous and self-sacrificing. If you attempt to determine her value from the natural perspective, you will miscalculate her price. After all, she was an orphan and a Jew. Her legal guardian was her cousin, Mordecai. She had no earthly riches, yet the king recognized that she was priceless. ***Gods Favour makes us priceless,*** far above rubies.

Esther had her name, her character, and her personality. She allowed God to use those attributes to bless her, and she willingly allowed God to use those same attributes to help her be a blessing to an entire Nation. Through her, the lives of all the Jews were saved (see the Book of Esther).

Outward beauty, with the nice hairdos, wearing of gold, and fine apparel, are not the attributes of a virtuous woman. The beauty must be in your heart, demonstrated in a gentle and quiet spirit. (1 Peter 3:3-4)

THE PROVERBS 31 MAN
11. The heart of her husband doth safely trust in her, so that he shall have no need of spoil.

The man described in this verse is a trusting man. He is secure in his wifes love. He doesnt just trust her, he safely trusts her. He has not misplaced his trust. He knows that he can safely trust her, because he trusts God and it was God who led him to her (Proverbs 3:5-6).

He is a confident man. He has made himself vulnerable to her. He has given her his heart. He is self-assured that she will protect his heart and all of the intimate things he has entrusted to her. He is a man who is not intimidated by a strong woman. He is a sensitive man. He recognizes that his woman is the cream of the crop and she produces the cream of the crop. She is an asset to him. She is not a brawling woman.

He is a satisfied man. Outside temptations do not entice him. He cannot be swayed, because he is satisfied. His love is steadfast and certain. He has no unmet needs.

AND HIS WOMAN
11. The heart of her husband doth safely trust in her, so that he shall have no need of spoil.

Elizabeth and her husband, Zacharias, were both righteous before God. Her husband was a Priest and she was a godly wife. They loved God and obeyed his commandments. Yet, despite their spiritual commitment to God, Elizabeth was barren. She could not conceive a child. Her situation temporarily clouded her judgment. She referred to her situation as a reproach. She did not see the HIGH calling of God in her life, even though her name meant, God is my oath. Her hope had diminished. Nevertheless, before the foundation of the world, God had planned that she would give birth to the forerunner of Jesus Christ, the Son of God. She had no way of knowing then, where God was taking her. However, there was a critical lesson to be learned. In order for her husbands heart to safely trust her, she had to learn to safely trust God. It is important that she passes the test.

One day Zacharias was in the Temple fulfilling his priestly duties, when an angel appeared to him. The angel told him that his wife, Elizabeth, was going to conceive a son and they should name him John. Because of their old age, Zacharias faith was temporarily shaken, and it resulted in him not being able to speak.

He came out of the Temple to the place where his wife and the congregation were waiting, but he was unable to talk. He shared what had happened in the Temple by writing it down. The crowd had opinions and reasons why the child should not be given the name spoken by the angel. Elizabeth was learning to trust. I will not go into the entire account, however, I present the following observations.

Most women who desire to express their opinions will do everything in their power to out-talk the man, including a raised volume in their voice. Yet, here is Zacharias, unable to talk and Elizabeth does not take advantage of the situation. She accepts what her husband says. She is demonstrating to her husband that he can safely trust her.

Which one of our modern day women would allow the man to name the baby that she had carried for nine months, without so much as consulting her or asking her opinion? Elizabeth didnt argue about the name, she simply accepted it and made it known to others that their sons name was John as her husband had written. The heart of Elizabeths husband safely trusted her even when he was most vulnerable (Luke 1).

THE PROVERBS 31 MAN
12. She will do him good and not evil all the days of her life.

This man has earned her loyalty, and there is nothing she wouldnt do for him. She makes sure he is comfortable. He is encouraged and built up by the things she does for him. He doesnt realize that he is responsible for her actions. He has been so good to her that *his wish is her desire!*

From the day that we were married until the present, my husband tells me, Honey, I want to be so good to you, that if something should happen and I become unable to do for myself, you will be glad to take care of me. Those words, along with his actions, are motivators for me to take care of him. He plants seeds into our marriage for that specific harvest. Unexpectedly and consistently, he fulfills my needs and desires. I can express a desire during a regular conversation, and before I know it, he has fulfilled that desire. His actions encourage my heart and cause me to want to do more and more for him. We have a multitude of stored up memories, one to the other.

In as much as he shares his desires, he shares his dislikes. One of his greatest pet peeves is selfishness. He constantly reminds me that when spouses love each other, they will seek to know what makes the other one happy. They will do everything in their power to fulfill the desires of the other. These types of things develop a sense of loyalty between spouses. Someone once said, Marriage is a total commitment, of a total life, for a total lifetime.

Doing him good and not evil shows that she knows and understands the purpose of marriage. She is his companion and not his slave. She is his partner and not his competitor. It is imperative that we appreciate our spouses value.

If there is conflict in the marriage, she will do him good and not evil. She will pray. She will trust. And even in the midst of their suffering, she will continue to believe that he is still worth all that she does and more.

Lets look at three ways to deal with conflict in marriage, realizing that only one is the right way:

❀ **Revenge**
Retaliation is not as sweet as some believe. The eye-for-an-eye mentality can destroy you and your marriage.

❀ **Withdrawal**
Physically and/or emotionally walking away and isolating one another is withdrawal. These acts of withdrawal will enable the enemy to successfully divide and conquer.

❀ **Honest and Loving Confrontation**
Doing it Gods way should lead to confession and repentance, which results in forgiveness. As we forgive, a healing will occur and the relationship will flourish as a result of the conflict.

In the not-so-distant past, I was cautioned against using the words confront or confrontation because of their negative connotation. However, I believe it is the motivation behind our actions, more so than merely using the words. The motivation should be to inspire, assist, or empower. Whether you call it confrontation or communication, it should be truthful, factual, and loving.

AND HIS WOMAN
12. She will do him good and not evil all the days of her life.

Often we look at people and because of who they are, we place them on pedestals. We tend to forget that people with high status have issues just like you and I. Sarah was a very beautiful woman. Her name meant Princess; Mother of Nations. Im sure you would agree she is a prime example of one with high status. Yet, she reverenced her husband and even called him, lord. While on the flip side, her husband dishonored her twice. He asked her to lie about their relationship. They were no longer half-brother and sister. They were husband and wife. The sibling relationship was dead. It died when they married. He not only risked their marriage relationship, he risked her being violated. Sarah loved her husband so much that she was willing to do whatever was good for him, all the days of her life. God seeing and knowing her heart intervened on her behalf each time. Now, this is the next level: Despite her husbands actions and choices, this Proverbs 31 Woman was always thinking about what she could do to please him, even in the Hagar saga. (Genesis 12-21)

THE PROVERBS 31 MAN
13. She seeketh wool, and flax, and worketh willingly with her hands.

This verse reveals that the Proverbs 31 Man is an encourager. There is something that this man has done to make his woman so willing to work, without regards to her possible limitations. He has probably spent his life loving, encouraging, and esteeming her above himself. And now, all she wants to do is try and measure up to his acts of love.

AND HIS WOMAN
13. She seeketh wool, and flax, and worketh willingly with her hands.

Ruth was a woman with vision. Her name meant Companion, Friend, Vision of beauty. She had learned the importance of vision from her mother-in-laws teachings. No doubt she had heard, If there is no vision, people will perish. Through her mother-in-laws teachings, she developed an alliance to her mother-in-laws God. Even though she was technically an outsider, her heart was committed to the true and living God and her mother-in-law. She eagerly assisted her mother-in-law.

When she counted the cost, she decided that she wanted to serve Naomis God no matter what. Ruths destiny hung on her seeking and working. She did it, and it paid off big time. She got Boaz. She was a Moabite, who married into a special family lineage, Jesus Christ (see the Book of Ruth).

There are single women who desire to have a husband; yet, little or no preparation is being made to receive their husband. They are looking for that perfect man to come along with his riches and take care of them. Its a pipe dream. However, there are single women who have their own riches, but cannot submit to Gods order. The best man she can get is the Proverbs 31 Man, and he has already been warned about both of these types.

THE PROVERBS 31 MAN

14. *She is like the merchants ships; she bringeth her food from afar.*

This verse presents a man who is secure. He knows in whom he believes. He trusts and respects the strength of his woman. He places no restraints on her. He allows her to travel alone and take care of business. She is a businesswoman who challenges, but does not intimidate. Her husband does not intimidate her at home, so when she leaves home she is not intimidated by her surroundings, or anyone she has to conduct business with.

AND HIS WOMAN

14. *She is like the merchants ships; she bringeth her food from afar.*

Tamar traveled some distance from **who she was** to get what she wanted. Her name meant Palm Tree. I can imagine her as a warm, but free-spirited woman. Without judging her, we can see that she had insight for business. She was the epitome of a wise businesswoman.

Tamar was the daughter-in-law of Judah, the King. Her first husband, Judahs eldest son, died, and she married the second oldest son. He rebelled against the Law of God, so God killed him. Nevertheless, Tamar was entitled to marry the third and last son of Judah, but he refused to give him to her. He told her to wait until the son was older. I can almost understand Judahs attempt to save his posterity. The survival rate for marriage with Tamar was pretty bleak. He was the King. And what king wouldn't want to groom his seed to replace him on the throne. Nevertheless, since Judah refused to give Tamar his last son, she took a detour and went to the streets. Although she was wrong in what she did, Judah was just as wrong in denying her his son. He was also as guilty as she for lying with her, thinking she was just another harlot.

Harlotry was not Tamars profession. Her business mind caused her to look beyond seeking revenge. Instead, she sought to rectify her situation. She just wanted to get what she was entitled to. It was a given, almost every woman wanted the chance to have a son who could possibly be the coming Messiah.

She was a visionary and a strategist. She looked at the price her action would cost her on **tomorrow.** Judah offered to pay her with a kid from his flock, for the services she had rendered. He promised to send the kid to her later. However, Tamar was thinking so far ahead of him that she asked for collateral. Her request was specific. She wanted his Signet, Bracelets, and Staff. I believe these items personified his power, authority, and his name. She now possessed the things that were important to him, even as he had held onto the son, which was important to her future. This was not revenge it was business! He was the King. If he had done something wrong, who was going to hold it to his charge? No one. Yet, he had her life and the life of all the people in the palm of his hands. And just as he was ready to have Tamar killed for playing the harlot and coming up pregnant, Tamar produced the collateral. She was a prudent woman (Genesis 38).

THE PROVERBS 31 MAN
15. She riseth also while it is yet night, and giveth meat to her household, and a portion to her maidens.

This man is living a stress-free life. And it is the Proverbs 31 Woman, who is seeing to it that no unnecessary stress comes his way. He lies down at night and gets some good sleep, because he trusts the person hes sleeping next to. He sleeps so soundly, that she quietly slips out of the bed, cooks breakfast, fixes lunch, and sets up a work plan for her maidens while he is still sleeping.

AND HIS WOMAN
15. She riseth also while it is yet night, and giveth meat to her household, and a portion to her maidens.

This Proverbs 31 Woman is not a procrastinator. She is not a time-waster. She uses her time management skills to get things done while others sleep. Those around her cannot understand how she gets so much accomplished. She requires little sleep. She willingly and happily ministers to her family. She makes it her business to do whatever is necessary, to ensure the happiness of her home. She is organized and keeps things in tact. She ensures that there is a separation of her home and her secular business. She is unselfish. Although she has maidens, she prefers to personally fulfill certain needs of her family. She respects her maidens and shows great hospitality towards them. When she prepares her spiritual and natural food for her family, she shares with her maidens. Any chores that reflect on her husband, she takes sole responsibility for doing them. She is an example to her household and her employees.

Eve is the Mother of ALL Living. Her name meant To breathe, To live. Where there is no life, she has the ability to produce life. Indulge me with this next statement. **Eve gave life to disobedience.** That life altered the operation of Gods order for man and woman. That life also brought death. Jesus came and realigned and reactivated Gods original order. Now this Proverbs 31 Woman is equipped and empowered to breathe life into everything she touches, but she does it with wisdom and discretion. She is so blessed that it is hard for her to stop blessing others.(Genesis 3)

THE PROVERBS 31 MAN
16. She considereth a field, and buyeth it: with the fruit of her hands she planteth a vineyard.

In every marriage, the strengths of each spouse may be different. It is great if the Proverbs 31 Man handles the finances of the household. However, if that is not his strength, it is not an indictment against him. He is even more honorable for recognizing that his wife is strengthened in this area, so he releases her to prosper.

Apparently, this man has discussed financial decisions with his wife. Because she is not required to return home before she can make a good purchase or business decision. She has been empowered. She is constantly considering the best way to improve their family life. She doesnt just buy. She buys and plants, working with her hands. She does all of this, but does not neglect any of her present duties.

AND HIS WOMAN
16. She considereth a field, and buyeth it: with the fruit of her hands she planteth a vineyard.

Naomi was a woman who took care of her household. Her husband ensured that she was knowledgeable about the affairs of the household. And he included her in the household decisions. Naomi's name meant Pleasantness. She understood the ways and heart of her husband. Yet, her husband carried the responsibility of the family. If her husband had not been the type of leader that he was, she would have been totally lost when he died. He led the family, but he helped her develop into the strong woman that she had become. She unexpectedly found herself as the head of the household. She had to make final decisions, which she was not required to do in the past. She rose to the occasion. And when her sons died, she took care of her daughters-in-law. When the daughters-in-law made their decisions, she **considered** Boaz's field, sent Ruth to his field, and there, manifold blessings awaited them (see the Book of Ruth).

THE PROVERBS 31 MAN
17. She girdeth her loins with strength, and strengtheneth her arms.

Although the Proverbs 31 Man recognizes that his woman is strong, he should still be considerate of her feelings and sensitive to her needs. He should treat her with respect as the weaker spouse, so that the progression of what she is trying to achieve would not be hindered. On a daily basis, she cares for her body, soul and spirit. She has her time of devotion with God.

She meditates on what God shares with her. And she does her physical exercises.

It doesnt matter how hard she works at it, she constantly battles with her weight. The birth of her children seemingly sabotaged her girlish figure, so she exercises. Then she stops, but she starts again; followed by another stop. Her Proverbs 31 Man is right there to strengthen her and encourage her to continue.

AND HIS WOMAN
17. She girdeth her loins with strength, and strengtheneth her arms.

Jael was a courageous woman. Her name meant Wild mountain goat.I envision her as a female warrior, ready for battle. While women today, including myself, run from mice, roaches, flies, bugs, etc., Jael was used by God to fulfill the Prophesy spoken by Deborah. Deborah told Barak that the Lord was going to deliver the enemy into the hands of a woman. Jael was that woman, waiting to fulfill the call of God in her life. Deborah was a woman of strength, walking in the power of God. Today our battle is not physical, but spiritual. We wrestle against the forces of darkness. Our weapons are the Word of God, intercessory prayer, and the Holy Spirit. Women are not ascribing to become super women, they are only trying to equip themselves for the call of God. (Judges 5:24-27)

THE PROVERBS 31 MAN
18. She perceiveth that her merchandise is good: her candle goeth not out by night.

This verse implies that the Proverbs 31 Man does not criticize his woman. He values her input and opinions. Because of the manner in which he deals with her, she is comfortable making decisions. She is confident that he will validate her decisions. She is so comfortable doing what she is doing, that she can almost do it in her sleep. When she should be in bed, she is strategizing. Her self-esteem is in tact, because he does not practice demeaning her. Even when she makes a bad decision he finds a way to make it all right.

AND HIS WOMAN
18. She perceiveth that her merchandise is good: her candle goeth not out by night.

Rizpah was a mother. Her name meant Hot Coal, Baking Stone. She was a passionate woman who was not easily swayed. She was focused and determined. Rizpah had two sons by Saul. Her sons were sons of a King. They were good merchandise. Good Stock! This mother refused to sleep until deliverance came to her sons.

She was so passionate about protecting her sons, that she protected them even in death. This all started because of a 3-year famine. During the famine, David, the King, asked the Gibeonites what would it take to get assistance from them. David learned that the Gibeonites were carrying a grudge against Saul, the former King who was now dead.

Even today, there are spouses who suffered with their spouse, but remained committed. However, after the spouse died, some of the things they did while they were alive still tormented the survivors. Every Proverbs 31 Man should do whatever it takes to ensure his Proverbs 31 Wife does not encounter this level of humiliation and embarrassment. I have attended funerals where children, women, money, and even secret families surfaced at death. This should never occur between The Proverbs 31 Man and His Woman. Become totally transparent with each other.

In this story, to appease their grudge, they asked David for the life of Sauls sons. They determined that nothing would compensate for the wrong Saul had done to them, except the death of Sauls seven sons.

After the Gibeonites killed them, they hung their bodies on public display. Rizpah positioned herself upon a rock near the hanging, and for months watched over the dead bodies of her children. She prevented them from being devoured by the beasts at night, and the fowls of the air during the day. She stayed there until King David granted her petition and her sons were taken down and buried. She refused to let her candle go out. (2 Samuel 21)

THE PROVERBS 31 MAN
19. *She layeth her hands to the spindle, and her hands hold the distaff.*

I believe the implication of this verse goes far beyond a stick, wool and thread.

Today, it is no surprise that men sew, as well as, women. Indulge me. I envision her husband as a Tailor. He is an expert in this arena. Nevertheless, he encourages her to create as much, and as often, as she likes. Apparels. Curtains. Bedspreads. Chair

Coverings. You name it. When she puts her mind to it, she makes it happen and hes right there encouraging her. Since his sewing skills are more advanced than hers, he willingly and patiently shares information with her and provides training as necessary.

AND HIS WOMAN
19. She layeth her hands to the spindle, and her hands hold the distaff.

This could have been a factory or a day laborer job, paying minimum wage. Regardless, the message is clear, she was not afraid of working hard. The Proverbs 31 Man can be confident that this woman will do whatever is necessary to have a happy home. She takes good care of her children. Her pride will not allow her to miss opportunities. Indulge me. This could also represent her past. She learns a skill while working for someone else. Then she creates her own business using the skills she acquired, and now she owns the company. She is self-employed and enjoying it.

This brings to mind Jochebed, Moses mother. Her name meant Glory of Jehovah. Having the glory of Jehovah upon her, she must have seen something different about her baby boy. Gods glory must have shone upon him. She couldnt explain the tugging she felt in her heart. She didnt know her eyes were beholding what would be one of the nations greatest leaders. She didnt know his future was dependent on how she handled the threat on his life. She placed her hands to the spindle and weaved a baby basket to preserve her sons life. She was courageous enough to take a risk, and confident enough to trust God. Her experience as a mother and nurse paid off. She became her sons nurse and was paid a salary for taking care of him. (Exodus 2)

THE PROVERBS 31 MAN
20. She stretcheth out her hand to the poor; yea, she reacheth forth her hands to the needy.

The Proverbs 31 Man may not understand where his woman finds the time or the strength to do all that she does. Nevertheless, he does not stand in the way of any thing she desires to do. He recognizes her love for the family and others. He is not at all threatened by her Outreach Ministry, helping others. He is supportive of all her efforts. He respects what she is doing, because he knows how she takes care of home. What she does for others, she does at home first.

AND HIS WOMAN
20. She stretcheth out her hand to the poor; yea, she reacheth forth her hands to the needy.

Abigail was an intelligent, beautiful, and wise woman. Her name meant, Cause of Joy. She used wisdom and discernment to save her family from destruction. Without charge, David and his army had protected Nabals possessions from the enemies. But when David asked for food, Nabal refused to give them any. In his anger, David was on his way to kill Nabal and everyone associated with him. They had sacrificially shown kindness to this man, and he denied them basics, which would have refreshed and strengthened them.

Every woman must know the man she is married to! And even when she is married to an arrogant fool, she can still be tenderhearted. Her kindness should be visible, inside and outside of the home. An unsaved husband can be won to Christ by the acts of a loving wife. However, if he rejects God, that loving wife is free from guilt.

Abigail is a good example of a loving wife. She had her own issues to deal with, but she found time to meet the needs of others, at the risk of getting into trouble with her husband. Abigail rushed to meet David. With persuasive words of wisdom and gifts of kindness, she averted the killing of her family. She met David with food and water in his hour of need. (1 Samuel 25)

THE PROVERBS 31 MAN
21. She is not afraid of the snow for her household: for all her household are clothed with scarlet.

There are leaders, and then, there are LEADERS! Leaders with vision and foresight are leaders who probably studied the ways of the ant, as they were instructed to do. This verse depicts a leader who knows the importance of advance preparations. This man does not know whether he will be alive tomorrow, but if tomorrow comes, and he or his loved ones are alive, he wants to be prepared. No doubt, as he talked with his wife informing her of his vision, and the direction the family should go in, she grasped the vision and ran with it.

AND HIS WOMAN
21. She is not afraid of the snow for her household: for all her household are clothed with scarlet.

This woman has followed her husbands lead. She has wisely planned for their future. She does not hoard, she prepares. When the crises of shelter, food, and clothing hit, her household will be prepared. While the hearts of many are fainting, she and her family will settle in and be cozy until the adverse situations end. Her house will be as the Hebrews houses, when the death angel came through Egypt. They will not fear because they are protected.

By now you should be absolutely convinced that the Proverbs 31 Woman is not afraid of hard work. She has learned that hard work pays off. She has realized great benefits from working hard.

Rebekah, whose name meant To Secure, received a marriage proposal because she was the right person, in the right place, at the right time, and joyfully working hard. While she was drawing water from the well, a thirsty stranger appeared and asked for a drink. Not knowing this special young man held her future in his hands, she happily gave him a drink and gave water to his camels also. Her unselfish acts resulted in her becoming a member of an elite family with a household filled with scarlet and a rich inheritance. (Genesis 24)

THE PROVERBS 31 MAN
22. She maketh herself coverings of tapestry; her clothing is silk and purple.

The Proverbs 31 Man has taken his identity seriously. He sees himself as a King and his wife as a Queen. He has spoken, lived, and operated on that level for so long, that everything else seems foreign. The fabrics of their life have been embroidered into a Royal status. They are enjoying the life intended for the Proverbs 31 Man and His Woman.

AND HIS WOMAN

22. She maketh herself coverings of tapestry; her clothing is silk and purple.

His wife is living the life that other women dream about. She is walking around in silk and purple. She is not arrogant or pretentious; rather, she is genuine and transparent. She has come a long way and she deserves every bite of it. She strolls and no one can stop her. She tilts her head and flashes a warm smile as she passes by. Onlookers acknowledge what she already knows, She is a Queen, and she has earned the title.

Hear Ye, Hear Ye, The Queen of Sheba! What do you envision when you hear that announcement? She was wealthy, beautiful, and powerful. She was a lady with more silk and purple than she could ever use; yet she found herself lacking in one area. It could have been devastating being the *crème de la crème* and learning that someone else had something that was more valuable than everything in your treasury. She is a Queen and she is a lady, so she is not devastated; instead, she is intrigued. She visits King Solomon. She must determine for herself if the rumors she heard about his wisdom were true. She showed up bearing gifts of great riches. She told King Solomon of the purpose for her visit. She had heard rumors and wanted to know whether they were true or not, and by the end of their meeting, she knew. She said, Not only do I believe, but the half was not told. Thy wisdom and thy prosperity exceed the rumors.

The Queen of Sheba returned satisfied. She wasn't out to get what he possessed. She wanted to know and understand The More Excellent Way. She sat and listened as he talked. She questioned everything. She wanted to know as much as he was willing to share. I believe she learned early in life that Iron sharpens iron. *She was a wise woman seeking to understand wisdom at a higher level.* Although he was blessed with great riches of his own, she blessed him with more riches. She wasnt trying to pay him, because what he imparted to her couldnt be priced; it was more valuable than silk and purple. (1 Kings 10)

THE PROVERBS 31 MAN
23. Her husband is known in the gates, when he sitteth among the elders of the land.

This verse portrays a proud man. He is not arrogant, just proud to be recognized and honored as the husband of a Proverbs 31 Wife. Although he is not an earthly king, he acts like one. Although he is not an elder, he sits among the elders. His wifes character has esteemed him. She has not done shameful acts, which would embarrass him, or cause him shame. He is highly esteemed because of her.

AND HIS WOMAN
23. Her husband is known in the gates, when he sitteth among the elders of the land.

She has represented him so well, that other men esteem him above themselves. They are one. The Proverbs 31 Man and His Woman are so united that when you see them, you see one! It was always her pleasure and goal to help him reach this status in life, and they are enjoying it together.

Rachel and Leah! One of their stories cannot be fully told without the other. Rachels name meant, Ewe, Little Lamb, symbolizing purity. She is described as beautiful and well-favoured. Conversely, Leahs name meant, Weary, Faint from

Sickness. In addition, she was tender-eyed. Tender-eyed has been translated into weak, nearsighted, bulging eyes, and cockeyed. So many people look at the beautiful outcome of a relationship, and think that it was always good. They dont realize that the final results are nothing more than the all things that worked together for the good, with God at the center. Though Jacob was named in the lineage of the forefathers, he became the father of the 12 Tribes of Israel because of both Leah and Rachel. Both of them are responsible for him being renown in biblical history.

Did you notice? I presented Rachel then Leah, and thats not the proper order. Most people do exactly what I did. They zero in on what appears beautiful and try to exclude the unattractive part. You decide, was Leahs heart more beautiful than Rachels?

THE PROVERBS 31 MAN
24. She maketh fine linen, and selleth it; and delivereth girdles unto the merchant.

This man has complimented his wife so much, that she is routinely making royal clothes for others. Teaching other women how to be a lady, a queen, and a handmaiden of the Lord. The more he compliments and encourages her, the more she finds to do. She doesnt wait for the merchants to request a shipment of her products, she delivers it to them in advance.

AND HIS WOMAN
24. She maketh fine linen, and selleth it; and delivereth girdles unto the merchant.

This wise woman is a designer. She designs things that are fashionable, yet, respectable. The garments she designs are fit for kings and queens. The aura of her designs commands attention. Yet, her fashions are not lewd or revealing.

Priscilla and her husband, Aquila, were tent makers by profession. Priscilla was talented and wise. She worked side-by-side with her husband every day. They also ministered together. Priscillas name meant, Primitive, Worthy, Respected. Today, some would dare say, It is old fashion for husbands and wives to work together. Others have gone further and said, It is not healthy for the marriage relationship to spend that much time together. You need breathing room, room to grow. Priscilla and Aquila are a testimony that the Proverbs 31 Man and His Woman can work, minister, and live together in peace all the days of their life. (Acts 18)

THE PROVERBS 31 MAN
25. Strength and honour are her clothing; and she shall rejoice in time to come.

You must see the man, behind the man. I believe every day, when this man rose up to dress himself, he first put on his invisible suit, the whole Armour of God. He was preparing to protect his woman. He was committed to covering her back. This Proverbs 31 Man was preserving the strength and protecting the honour of his Proverbs 31 Woman.

AND HIS WOMAN
25. Strength and honour are her clothing; and she shall rejoice in time to come.

Deborah! Deborah! Deborah! Her name meant, Bee. She personified the term, busy as a bee Deborah was unstoppable. She was a woman of excellence. She was the first and only woman Judge of Israel. She was also a Prophetess and a wife. She was a leader who was respected and admired. In strength and honour, she fulfilled the requirements of each office. She settled disputes. She accompanied Barak, the Commander-in-chief of the soldiers, to battle. Barak refused to go to battle without Deborah. He knew that her presence would bring victory. This has nothing to do with, nor in support of womens lib. This has to do with Gods Presence being so strong in our lives that it shines through us, brings us victories, and sends glory to God. (Judges 4-5)

THE PROVERBS 31 MAN
26. She openeth her mouth with wisdom; and in her tongue is the law of kindness.

I believe this man has successfully completed the Proverbs 31 Man and His Woman Training. No doubt he shared the insights with his wife as he went along; and as his wisdom developed, so did hers. They grew and matured together.

Throughout this last and final chapter, I have presented biblical examples to illustrate my points and beliefs. However, I know that there are living examples of Proverbs 31 Men and Women walking among us today. This brings to mind, a Proverbs 31 Man, Bishop Carlis L. Moody Sr. He did not complete the

Proverbs 31 Man and His Woman Training *per se.* Yet, **he is a personification of the Proverbs 31 Man.**

His absentee father did not teach him, and his working mother could not teach him all that he needed. He received limited help from leaders and mentors. It took God, through His Word and the Holy Spirit, to fully and completely teach him how to become a Proverbs 31 Man.

From a young boy his grandmother, MaDear, wallpapered the ceiling of his bedroom with pages out of old Sunday school books. He untiringly read those pages day and night. He developed an undying love for the Word of God, memorizing Scriptures from Genesis to Revelation. The Word of God taught him how to be a godly, wise, just, and prudent man. Although not perfect, with each new circumstance he gains more spiritual insight and continues to grow wiser. He routinely shares his wisdom with his Proverbs 31 Wife. He teaches her the things the Holy Spirit teaches him. I believe his Curriculum from Genesis to Revelation was more advanced and aggressive than The Proverbs 31 Man and His Woman Training Program. Bishop Moody has dedicated his life to teaching and training men and women, young and old, the principles contained in the Book of Proverbs.

This Proverbs 31 Man and His Woman have lived, witnessed, and proven the truths contained in this book. Bishop and Mother Moodys relationship has been the standard by which so many men and women measure their relationships, and they continue to raise the bar. A Proven Proverbs 31 Man!

AND HIS WOMAN
26. She openeth her mouth with wisdom; and in her tongue is the law of kindness.

This Proverbs 31 Woman is a *force* to be reckoned with. Dont let the soft-spoken, warm touch, and beautiful smile mislead you. She is an Esther, Abigail, and Deborah wrapped up in one, Mother Mary A. Moody. She enjoys the time her Proverbs 31 Man shares with her imparting spiritual insights. She ponders his words in her heart and adds them to that which she already possesses.

She is a **Powerhouse** filled with wisdom and kindness. She is in great demand. Because of her wisdom, women from all walks of life desire to spend time with her and be taught by her. Every woman who encounters her, walks away feeling special and thinking she is the preferred one. Little does each of them know, every woman whom this Proverbs 31 Woman touches, feels that special way. She has grown and matured in wisdom along with her Proverbs 31 Man. She is equipped to handle any situation, big or small. She is a realist and she touches you where you are.

I said earlier, Every woman must know the man she is married to. This Proverbs 31 Woman knows her husband. Many years ago, I was in the midst of a fiery trial, fighting to keep my spirit alive. I had been fasting for several days. I went to church and encountered the **Powerhouse.** She began to encourage me. Out of her mouth came wisdom, and her tongue was the law of kindness. I was explaining how I felt in my spirit from the fasting, and she took it and ran with it. She said, I know what you are saying, you feel clean. Thats how I feel about Honey. He is a clean man This floored me! I never saw it coming, but I never forgot it. Women dont routinely describe their husbands virtue! They draw your attention to their physical attributes. This Proverbs 31 Virtuous Woman knows Her Proverbs 31 Virtuous Man.

THE PROVERBS 31 MAN
27. She looketh well to the ways of her household, and eateth not the bread of idleness.

This is all about the environment that this man has established in his home. He is the leader in his home. He does not leave any thing to care for itself. He teaches his family the ways of his household. He reminds them that the devil uses an idle mind, so they should always be doing something productive. This man is undoubtedly a hard worker. His actions are reflective of the standards he has established for his household. He does not sit around and allow his household to fall apart. He immediately fixes what needs to be fixed. He replaces what needs to be replaced. And he destroys what needs to be destroyed. His wife has observed him. His actions support his teachings. He influences his wife and she follows his lead. She does not waste time gossiping or engaging in negativity. She is busy.

AND HIS WOMAN
27. She looketh well to the ways of her household, and eateth not the bread of idleness.

The Shunammite woman was a wealthy and well-respected person in her community. She had a kind and thankful heart. Her name is unknown but her character is filled with compassion. She was a visionary, who knew how to maintain her wealth. Her secret was giving; planting seeds in other peoples lives. She took care of Elisha, the Man of God. She fed him and had a room built for him in her house. She told Elisha she did not need or want anything in return. She was contented and happy. But he prophesied that she would have a son, and she did. She received increased wealth that she did not work for, because she was not a woman of idleness! (2 Kings 4:8-37)

THE PROVERBS 31 MAN
28. Her children arise up, and call her blessed; her husband also, and he praiseth her.

This man is proud of his wife and children. He looks forward to people meeting and interacting with his wife and children. In the absence of his wife, he proudly places his children on display. He talks about them and their accomplishments so much, that there is always someone desiring to meet them. Usually after their interactions with others, the children would be complimented regarding their mannerism and behavior. In his response, he accredits their stellar behavior to his wife. He acknowledges the work she has done. He praises her and makes sure everyone knows that his wife does what she does with her whole heart, and without any strings attached. He seals his praise with, I indeed found my Proverbs 31 Woman.

AND HIS WOMAN
28. Her children arise up, and call her blessed; her husband also, and he praiseth her.

Hannah was one of Elkanah's two wives. Elkanah loved Hannah more than he loved his other wife, Peninnah. But Hannah was barren. Since Peninnah had children, she mocked Hannah daily. Hannah was never envious. Her name meant Favour or

Grace. In the midst of her troubles, she continually prayed to God. Her wisdom to pray produced great results. She received the favor of God. None of Peninnahs children was renown, but Hannahs son, Samuel, was. He became a prophet and judge in Israel. I believe Samuel becoming a renowned prophet and judge, also made Hannah very popular. His *raised* status brought her praise. (1 Samuel 1-2)

THE PROVERBS 31 MAN
29. Many daughters have done virtuously, but thou excellest them all.

This man never stops moving forward. And his wife is right there beside him. They realize that there is still a lot of ground left to cover. They will not stop along the way to pick flowers, which will wither and die. They keep raising the bar of excellence. There are others who are good, but this man and woman have gone beyond good. They are wise. They operate daily on a life-long theme they were taught, Teach a wise man and he will be yet wiser.

AND HIS WOMAN
29. Many daughters have done virtuously, but thou excellest them all.

This woman does not compare herself to other women. She knows, to do so, is a lack of wisdom. She directs her attention to the potential inside of her, and determines what is needed to bring it forth. She will not allow it to remain inside of her and die.

Mary, a virgin, was called of God to give birth to the Son of God, Jesus. From an early age her life was filled with faith, love, and virtue. However, she was poor according to the worlds standards. Nevertheless, this poor woman exceeded all the women before her. I dont know about her appearance, but I do know that her character received *Gods Seal of Approval.* When the angel spoke with Mary, he said, Hail Mary, thou art highly favored, blessed art thou among women. Every woman who is a child of God is highly favored and is a blessed woman. Yet, the question remains, Will she excel? (Luke 1-2)

THE PROVERBS 31 MAN
30. Favour is deceitful, and beauty is vain: but a woman that feareth the LORD, she shall be praised.

Compliments, whether genuine or fake do not move this man. He has learned that the favour of man is deceitful, and beauty in its most elegant state is vain. The most secure thing in his life is his reverence of God. He stands steadfast on the Word of God, and he has a wife who reverently fears God. She is praised daily!

AND HIS WOMAN
30. Favour is deceitful, and beauty is vain: but a woman that feareth the LORD, she shall be praised.

Rahab was a prostitute and no doubt beautiful. Her house was located on the wall of the city. It was the ideal location for her profession. Rahab had heard of the God of Israel and she feared Him. This woman whose entire life centered around deceit, beauty, and vanity, suddenly realized that these things could not help her. Her name meant Proud; but the time came when she had to set her pride aside and use her faith. She used her faith to help the men of God, which later saved her entire household. Her act of faith and decision to follow God brought her full-circle into the lineage of Jesus Christ. She became a woman who feared God and worthy to be praised. (Joshua 2)

THE PROVERBS 31 MAN
31. Give her of the fruit of her hands; and let her own works praise her in the gates.

This verse reveals a man who is strong in his faith and confident in his manhood. He does not hesitate to give his wife credit for what she has done. He is not ashamed to publicly talk about the things she has done to help him. He knows that he has become an even better man, because he listened to her wisdom. He recalls the times her intervention kept them from great losses. Seeing the results of her work in their home makes him eager to tell everyone about her. All he needs is a listening ear. He is willing to shout it from the rooftop. He wants to give her, whats due her.

AND HIS WOMAN
31. Give her of the fruit of her hands; and let her own works praise her in the gates.

This woman did it for all of the right reasons. She continued doing it because lives were being changed. She expanded it to fulfill needs. She doesnt depend on others to encourage her. She simply looks at the works of her hands, and smiles. She is a satisfied woman, and doesnt take anything for granted. She is comforted in knowing that she has been blessed with a Proverbs 31 Man, and her life can only get better, so finally, She Rests!

THE PROVERBS 31 MAN AND HIS WOMAN

In the whole scheme of things, everything that a husband or a wife does for each other should be ***done out of reverence to God.*** This applies to both the spiritual and natural. This is what further develops and matures the virtuous man and virtuous woman.

Be reminded that maturity comes with many faces. It may even come in the midst of our difficult and troubled times. Priceless lessons are learned in difficult times. Although pain may temporarily block our *view,* our resolve will cause our *vision* to grow stronger, if we see things through Gods eyes. We must see the unseen, the invisible, and the eternal! ***Look beyond yourself and your situation, and see what is really real.***

THERE IS A PROVERBS 31 MAN IN YOU!

31 FAITH CONFESSIONS OF A PROVERBS 31 MAN

I AM...

1. A God-fearing man
2. A man who obeys God's Word
3. A righteous man
4. A wise man
5. A man of integrity
6. A holy man
7. A man who controls his temper
8. A truthful man
9. A kind man
10. A just man
11. An honest man
12. A compassionate man
13. A hardworking man
14. A forgiving man
15. A man who admits being wrong
16. A generous man
17. A sensitive man
18. A good man
19. A clean man
20. A positive man
21. A peacemaker
22. A trusting man
23. A gentle man
24. A faithful man
25. A disciplined man
26. A dependable man
27. A man who cares about others
28. An honorable man
29. A man abiding in favor
30. A diligent man
31. A prudent man

THE PROVERBS 31 MAN AND HIS WOMAN

GROWING TOGETHER

INSTRUCTIONS: Each verse of Proverbs 31:10-31 first describes the Proverbs 31 Man and then the verse is repeated describing the Proverbs 31 Woman. After you have read this section individually, read it together following these instructions. Using the descriptions cited each spouse should complete the following Action for each verse.

ACTION: The Man reads aloud the Womans description, discusses the attributes identified, and encourages his wife in light of the truths presented. Pointing out her similarities to the Woman being described. Afterwards, gently discuss the areas in her life, which you would desire to see enhanced. Read the verses in sequential order and complete one verse at a time for both the Man and the Woman.

Reverse the roles and the Woman reads aloud the Mans description, discusses the attributes identified, and encourages her husband in light of the truths presented. Pointing out his similarities to the Man being described. Afterwards, gently discuss the areas in his life, which you would desire to see enhanced. Read the verses in sequential order and complete one verse at a time for both the Man and the Woman.

APPENDIX

❧

1. In your own words explain the objective of this Training Manual.

   _____

   _____

2. The foundation of life starts with_____

3. To become a successful Proverbs 31 Man, you must _____
   _____, _____, and
   _____ by the principles of Proverbs.

4. An authentic Proverbs 31 Man is not_____
   by his Proverbs 31 Woman.

5. Explain in your own words why it is so critical for the instruction of a father and the law of a mother to be in sync.

   _____

   _____

6. Mom is the epitome of the _____
   and the _____

7. Dont join your _____or your _____
   _____with sinners.

8. A Proverbs 31 Man lives _____
    and operates in _____

9. True or False: Temptation customizes itself for its victim.
    (Explain your answer)

    _____

    _____

10. The Proverbs 31 Man consistently chooses the path of
    _____ and not the path of _____

11. Your _____ and your _____
    are essential to successfully complete the Proverbs 31 Mans
    Training.

12. Wisdom is a _____ that you must seek
    and search for.

13. Two types of wisdom were discussed. They are _____
    _____ and _____

14. _____ is the principal thing.

15. Wisdom is a _____ process.

16. Wisdom will help you _____
    _____, _____
    _____, and _____

17. Three characteristics of a Proverbs 31 Mans life are:
    _____, _____, and _____

18. C_____ and C_____
    are other methods of teaching and training.

19. A Proverbs 31 Man must maintain a _____
    _____

20. What is the Additive to Wisdom? _____

21. How important is the fathers teachings in future generations?
    Why?
    _____
    _____

22. What is the benefit of telling others the things your father
    told you?
    _____
    _____

23. If you had to describe what *Wisdom* looks like, what would
    be your description? Why?
    _____
    _____

24. Guard your _____ against evil.

25. What is as sweet as a honeycomb and smoother than oil?
    _____
    _____

26. What does Drink waters out of your own cistern mean to
    you?
    _____

27. What is the price of a rendezvous with a prostitute?

_____

_____

28. What is the benefit of a warning?

_____

_____

29. Share a warning you received, whether you ignored it or obeyed it, and what were the final results.

_____

_____

30. List the pros and cons of co-signing for another persons debt.

_____

_____

31. What are some signs/criterion that identifies a healthy 2-way friendship/relationship?

_____

_____

32. Meditate on your closest relationship and determine whether it is a healthy 2-way relationship/friendship.

_____

_____

33. Think about your areas of challenge and identify what you can learn from the ant.

_____

_____

34. List the things that God hates, AND look inward to see if any of them are within you.

_____

_____

35. What is the thing, which is an abomination to God? Is it in you?

_____

_____

36. What is the chief separator of family and friends?

_____

_____

37. Without purpose, laziness still produces results, list some.

_____

_____

38. _____ will lead you when you walk, keep you when you sleep, and talk with you when you are awake.

39. What can bring a man down to A piece of bread?

_____

_____

40. Who is on the prowl to destroy your clean and precious life?

_____

_____

41. Explain why continuous lighthearted interactions with the opposite gender can become destructive to your relationship.

_____

_____

42. What is the thing that can destroy your soul?_____

43. Identify ways to get the message of this Training Manual to the next generation.

_____

_____

44. List lies about life that the enemy is telling the next generation.

_____

_____

45. How different are those lies from the ones you were told?

_____

_____

46. Tell the young men to close their _____ and _____ to the voice of the _____

47. Only the strong survived because _____

_____

48. What must you consistently maintain when opportunity knocks?

_____

_____

49. In your own words, explain the importance of moral principles.

_____

_____

50. If you have ever gone against your morals, how did you feel afterwards?

_____

_____

51. Your landmarks of life should be your _____

_____

52. Correcting your children can deliver them from _____

_____

53. What are some of the rewards of Wisdom?

_____

_____

54. In your own words, explain the rewards of listening to the counsel of old parents.

_____

_____

55. You know you are becoming a Proverbs 31 Man when you can say what to your son?

_____

_____

56. Who is described as a deep ditch that you should avoid?

_____

_____

57. Discuss why the emotional areas listed in Proverbs 23:29 make the Man vulnerable.

_____

_____

58. What emotion is called the green-eyed monster, and why is it so dangerous?

_____

_____

59. List the things you need to change in order to become a fully equipped Proverbs 31 Man.

_____

_____

60. Using your list above, will you establish a goal to become a Proverbs 31 Man by a specific date?

_____

_____

61. How can what you know about evil help you to become a Proverbs 31 Man?

_____

_____

62. List some of the ways of the Wise.

_____

_____

63. Wisdom will teach you to _____
    and _____ evil things.

64. How influential are your friends to you becoming a Proverbs 31 Man? (Explain)

_____

_____

65. True or False: God has ordained you to be a Proverbs 31 Man.

PROVERBS 31 MAN AND HIS WOMAN ANSWER KEY

1. Your Own Words
2. God
3. Listen, Learn, Live
4. Intimidated
5. Your Own Words
6. Law of Love; Fountain of Life
7. Hand; Heart
8. Peaceably; Truth
9. True
10. Life; Death
11. Ears; Heart
12. Treasure
13. Worldly; Godly
14. Wisdom
15. Life-long
16. Detect Evil Motives; Evaluate Actions; Identify Consequences
17. Mercy; Truth; and Trust
18. Chastisement; Correction
19. Teachable Spirit
20. Discretion
21. Your Own Words
22. Your Own Words
23. Your Own Words
24. Heart
25. An Enticing Womans Lips and the Words, which come out of her mouth.
26. Your Own Words
27. A Destroyed Life
28. Your Own Words
29. Your Own Words
30. Your Own Words
31. Your Own Words
32. Your Own Words
33. Your Own Words

34. A Proud Look; A Lying Tongue; Hands that Shed Innocent Blood; A Heart that Devise Wicked Imaginations; Feet that are Swift in Running to Mischief; and a False Witness that Speaks Lies. (Conduct your private Self-Examination)
35. The Person who Sows Discord Among Brethren.
36. Money/Co-Signing
37. Your Own Words
38. Wisdom
39. A Whorish Woman
40. The Adulteress
41. Your Own Word
42. Committing Adultery
43. Your Own Words
44. Your Own Words
45. Your Own Words
46. Hearts; Ears; Adulteress
47. They Kept the Law of God on the table of their hearts
48. Your Character
49. Your Own Words
50. Your Own Words
51. Memorials of Truth
52. The Wrong Path
53. Your Speech is with Wisdom; You Reverence God, Your Expectations will not be Cut Off
54. Your Own Words
55. Give Me Your Heart and Watch My Life
56. A Whore
57. Your Own Words
58. Envy
59. Your Own Words
60. Your Own Words
61. Your Own Words
62. You dont have respect of persons, in judgment,
    You dont call the wicked, righteous,
    You support the person who answers in truth,
    You prepare for work,

You prioritize your home and business,
You are not a false witness,
You are not deceptive,
You dont seek revenge, and,
You pay every man according to his work.
63. Discern; Recognize
64. Your Own Words
65. AMEN!!!

JUST THE TWO OF US

Directions: Couples can use this, OR it can be used in a group setting.

STRENGTHENING OUR RELATIONSHIP

1. In one minute, name as many positive qualities as you can about your spouse.

2. On a piece of paper, rate your marriage relationship using numbers from 1 to 10, with 10 being the highest ranking. Then add your rankings together and divide by 2. The resulting number will represent the size of your relationship challenge. Openly and honestly discuss the size of your challenge, the issues and concerns, and some remedies.

3. Who/What do you believe your spouse has the greatest devotion to? (i.e., God, dad, mom, you, sports, child, self, etc.)

4. *REFLECTION*When you have grown in years, what memories from your marriage you believe you will reflect back on the most? Why?

5. What was it about your spouse that made you fall in love with her or him?

6. *IMAGINE:* You and your spouse standing between two worlds, natural and spiritual, you must fulfill the requirements for both worlds. Your goal is to move forward together. What would you need your spouse to help you with in both worlds to enable you to fulfill the requirements? For example:
   My husband is a buffer for meNatural
   My husband is an encouragerSpiritual

This exercise is simply for you to share with your spouse the area in which you need them the most, both naturally and spiritually.

7. **SAFELY TRUST**This is the highest level of trust, and it is a productive trust. It produces what is needed! Share with each other the first time you experienced a Safe Trust in your relationship. If you have not had this experience, share what needs to be done for you to experience safe trust.

8. Someone once said, Leave things better than you found them. With that statement in mind, discuss that thing your spouse desires to see change, but you have not done so; and if you were honest, you would admit that it is a small thing in comparison to a lifetime relationship.

9. Discuss and come to a consensus as to what aspect of your marriage reflects the image of Christ the most, the thing that makes God smile.

10. What is your rotational schedule for renewing your vows with your spouse? (daily, weekly, monthly, quarterly, yearly, never)Spouses need reassurance. Discuss starting one.

11. How often do you and your spouse attend a Marriage Retreat/Conference? Discuss whether you think they are necessary. Why or why not?

12. Are you and your spouse each others best friend? Why or why not?

13. From 1 to 5, indicate Gods order for your home; arrange in priority order (Family, Church/Ministry, God, Government, Marriage).

14. What is your spouses favorite color?

15. What is your spouses favorite food or dessert?

BONUS: Has the chivalrous man in YOU disappeared behind the automatic car remote? Do you click it, the doors unlock, and your Proverbs 31 Woman is forced to fend for herself? Most, if not all, spouses still appreciate having their doors opened for them. (DISCUSS)

BOOKS written by Rena Boston

Walking Softly I $12.95

A book of poetry designed to help keep love alive. It creates an intimate ambiance to discuss ugly issues and helps men and women express their feelings. It brings warmth to ice cold settings. This book is a must read...(June 2003)

Walking Softly II $12.95

Part Two of the Walking Softly Book Collection reveals new ideas to invigorate your relationship. It is for anyone who is "in love", waiting "for love", and those who are not sure "about love". (August 2004)

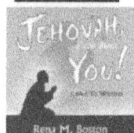

Jehovah, It's All About You-Book $7.95

Have you ever been Center-Stage with God? Use this book during your devotions and it will move you into a powerful worship experience with God. (September 2004)

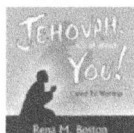

Jehovah, It's All About You-CD $15.00

This CD contains the Jehovah worship book PLUS several worship songs intermittently sung by Renown Artist, Kenneth L. Daniel. Allow this CD to move you into a powerful worship experience with God. (June 2005)

"If Only" Motivational CD $7.00

Have you ever made excuses you knew were unacceptable? After all, self-preservation is all about excuses; our reasons and justifications for "doing" and "saying"; what we do and say. Stop allowing excuses to stunt your growth! (June 2005)

Walking Softly Calendar $12.95

This calendar contains 12 poems surrounding love-walking. The power to feel love, find love, and experience love are on every page. The monthly challenges are designed to create an atmosphere of sensitivity and warmth. (October 2005)

BOOKS written by Rena Boston

Humility Before Honour $19.95

This hardcover book is a must read. It is a "keepsake" for generations to come. Bishop Carlis Lee Moody, Sr.'s biography will reveal a man of faith and integrity. He has travelled the globe fulfilling the great commission in over 42 countries. He is an international symbol of hope to those he serves. (October 2005)

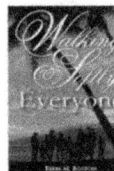

Walking Softly for Everyone $14.95

This book contains a special message for everyone. It encourages the discouraged, cautions the singles, massages the heart of the divorced, and prepares the married for a life of challenge and love. (April 2007)

HOPES DREAMS VISIONS $9.95

This motivational handbook revitalizes the heart, and provides strength to conquer obstacles in life. It contains 60 scenarios designed to elevate the readers' expectations of themselves. (August 2013)

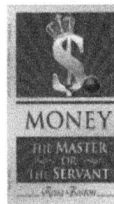

MONEY, the MASTER or the SERVANT $8.95

This book is a must-read! However, you may find yourself laughing and crying at the same time. It may even feel like a roller coaster ride, but I assure you there's a safe landing. It is designed to motivate you to become the Master of your Money and sharpen your awareness of money's proper place as a Servant. Learn how to allow your money to serve you. As you stroll with me on this debt- free journey, you will experience a liberation and a thirst to assume control of your money immediately. The primary goal of this book is to encourage you to begin your debt-free journey by managing your money wisely. (10/29/14)

BOOKS written by Rena Boston

NO SCARS $11.95

Raven was on the verge of insanity; yet, she escaped with 'No Scars'. The evidence of her sufferings was wiped away. It was so dramatic that it was almost unbelievable. Slowly stepping forward, Raven contemplated her image in the mirror. The reflection she saw and its persona overwhelmed her. She did not look like what she had gone through! She didn't even look like her original image, she was better! (1/20/15)

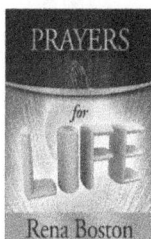

PRAYERS for LIFE $11.95

This book was written to promote prayer in our daily lives. It contains fully scripted Bible-based, faith-filled prayers. The theme is: "Prayer is to our spirit, what breath is to the body; LIFE!" (4/12/16)

Just Writers Publishing Company
"Where Fingers Write From the Heart"

*Prices do not include Shipping & Handling.

www.ingramcontent.com/pod-product-compliance
Lightning Source LLC
Chambersburg PA
CBHW032037040426
42449CB00007B/928